THE WASHINGTON PAPERS
Volume VII

∂84-∂BE-131
628 range

69: THE UNITED STATES AND KOREA
Looking Ahead

Robert A. Scalapino

Preface by Ray S. Cline

THE CENTER FOR STRATEGIC AND INTERNATIONAL STUDIES
Georgetown University, Washington, D.C.

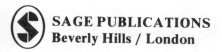

SAGE PUBLICATIONS
Beverly Hills / London

For information address:

SAGE PUBLICATIONS, INC.   SAGE PUBLICATIONS LTD
275 South Beverly Drive   28 Banner Street
Beverly Hills, California 90212   London EC1Y 8QE

International Standard Book Number 0-8039-1374-5

Library of Congress Catalog Card No. 79-54241

FIRST PRINTING

---

*When citing a Washington Paper, please use the proper form. Remember to cite the
series title and include the paper number. One of the two following formats can be
adapted (depending on the style manual used):*

(1) HASSNER, P. (1973) "Europe in the Age of Negotiation." The Washington
Papers, I, 8. Beverly Hills and London: Sage Pubns.

OR

(2) Hassner, Pierre. 1973. *Europe in the Age of Negotiation*. The Washington Papers,
vol. 1, no. 8. Beverly Hills and London: Sage Publications.

CONTENTS

PREFACE

Recent rapid changes in the security relationships among nations in Northeast Asia require careful reassessment of the main issues of American foreign policy concerning the region and, in particular our longtime ally, the Republic of Korea. Dr. Scalapino examines the regional strategic context and bilateral Korean-American problems in detail in order to discover why there has been a marked deterioration during the past few years in the close cooperation that characterized relations between Washington and Seoul for about a quarter century. American troops withdrawals, the military threat from North Korea, the Carter administration's heavy emphasis on human rights, and the thorny political interactions between Seoul and Washington described as "Koreagate" are all carefully and objectively assessed.

In addition, the author outlines the temptations and the dangers of bilateral American negotiations with the Communist regime in North Korea, and describes the impact of the policies of Japan, the People's Republic of China (PRC), and the Soviet Union on the situation in both parts of the Korean peninsula. The strategic importance of South Korea as the center of conflicting forces from all these countries, all bearing on the Republic of Korea and trying to pressure it in different directions, is amply demonstrated in this thoughtful look at the present and the future of the whole Northeast Asian region.

Dr. Scalapino clearly demonstrates that the Republic of Korea is a nation important in its own right and crucial to the strategic stability of the region. He argues persuasively that with so many uncertainties about Soviet, PRC, Japanese, and North Korean intentions in the future, the United States ought to steer a steady policy course in the area with strong and visible guarantees of the security and economic and political stability of South Korea.

This authoritative review of the complex mix of problems in Northeast Asia provides an excellent basis for the policy debates on Korea that are likely to be taking place in the next decade. The study was conducted as part of the Center's World Power Assessment program, made possible by a grant from the Sarah Scaife Foundation.

Ray S. Cline
Executive Director
World Power Studies

I. RECENT SECURITY RELATIONS

American-Korean relations in the recent past have been a mirror to a much broader set of issues, domestic as well as international. They are a graphic illustration of the fact that no specific bilateral relationship can be separated from the wider context in which it operates. American troop withdrawal: was it not perceived as closely connected with the Vietnam debacle? "Koreagate": did it not represent a Korean evaluation of both the threat of an American retreat and of "standard political practices," American as well as Korean? Human rights: was a progressive liberalization of Korean society likely, given its political culture and geopolitical position, as the American presence in East Asia weakened?

Presumably, no one would deny that relations between the United States and the Republic of Korea deteriorated up to 1979. We have already signaled some of the principal issues, but it is necessary to set forth somewhat more fully the nature and scope of the deterioration before surveying future prospects. No nation was affected more by the American abandonment of Vietnam than Korea. Aside from the Americans the Koreans had been the one outside force of significant size seeking to aid the non-communist cause in Vietnam. In Seoul, beyond the loss of face involved in this ignominious defeat, the temptation was overwhelming to see a rolling American strategic withdrawal from Asia.

Indeed, as early as 1969, President Pak Chŏng-hi privately indicated that he regarded such a withdrawal as inevitable, and he voiced anxiety as to whether time would be granted to Korea to adjust to the new era. The Guam Doctrine could be read in various ways, and Pak chose to accept an interpretation that involved a large-scale American cut-back. He and many other Koreans quickly sensed that the American people, in the aftermath of their first major political-military defeat in modern times, were weary of international commitments and surfeited with domestic problems. Apprehensions rose when the United States made a decision in the spring of 1970 to withdraw 20,000 troops from South Korea. Thus, when Vice President Agnew visited Seoul in August 1970, he was presented with a series of requests from President Pak, including the demand for a written guarantee that the United States would fight to defend Korea, that no additional American troops would be withdrawn, and that the United States would provide $3 billion in military assistance over the succeeding 5 years (Halloran, 1977). Agnew could only promise that the U.S. government would seek congressional support for additional military assistance and emphasize the limitations upon independent administrative actions of the type requested, thereby laying the ground for the subsequent efforts of South Korea to win support from Congress and influential Americans.

When Jimmy Carter pledged an American troop withdrawal from Korea during the 1976 Presidential campaign, therefore, it did not come as a novel or wholly unexpected proposal. Nevertheless, disappointment and a sharp rise in the level of anxiety were registered in Seoul. The Ford administration had put withdrawal on the shelf, prepared to wait for a more propitious time. Nor had this issue been coupled with the human rights question earlier, a development adding to the uncertainties surrounding American intentions.

The case for the withdrawal of American ground forces from Korea had long been articulated, with one dominant, central theme. Since the involvement of large numbers of American ground forces in an Asian conflict was no longer feasible politically nor necessary militarily, it would be wise to prepare our allies for new limits upon American assistance. Such preparation—psychological as well as military—could best be achieved as on-going American military commitments were adjusted to the political-strategic realities that would govern any future conflict. Only in this fashion could governments like the Republic of Korea be better prepared to cope with the requirements that would be thrust upon them in the event of war. Since the American position in Korea was a particularly exposed one, the sooner the adjustments, the better for all concerned.

It was also suggested that troop withdrawal would contribute to a sense of Korean self-reliance, stimulating a greater responsibility, without disturbing the American pledge to fulfill its treaty commitments in the event of an attack. Would not the projected use of American air and sea power serve to deter any North Korean aggression?

Responses to these arguments were not lacking. It was asserted that even a small number of American troops served two vital purposes. First, they made the American commitment totally credible, and hence, the threat of any North Korean aggression absolutely minimal. To retreat from this position raised risks, particularly the threat of an assault limited to the "liberation" of Seoul, pursued with the utmost speed and followed by the effort to involve the South Korean government and others in political negotiations, with the advantages of a superior bargaining position. Why should the *raison d'etre* of ground forces be less meaningful with respect to Korea than in the case of Western Europe?

In Korea, moreover, American forces had been important in defusing incidents which, had they occurred in a setting involving only North and South Koreans, could easily have escalated into large-scale conflict. The axe murders of August 1976, for example, might well have resulted in violence approximating war, with the United States being forced to make exceedingly painful decisions in a situation over which its control was limited.

Clearly, there were no economic advantages in the troop withdrawal unless demobilization were contemplated, since the soldiers could not be maintained more cheaply elsewhere. And while a growing self-reliance on the part of the Koreans was desirable and inevitable—given economic and political trends—a proper timing of American reductions was critical. Otherwise, feelings of insecurity might well outweigh all other emotions, with actions in the political and strategic realm attuned to such feelings. In such a case, the immediate future of political liberalization promised to be dim, and at what point might the temptation to move toward nuclear weapons be translated into active initiatives?

In sum, it was asserted that the risks involved in an American troop withdrawal far outweighed those involved in the maintenance of current policies, at least under prevailing circumstances.

The above lines of argument represented the main area of dispute, but there were other issues of a broader, more philosophic nature that served to shape opinions on both sides. Supporting the arguments for withdrawal, a certain body of American opinion advanced the following thesis: in addition to the fact that the injunction against involving the United States strategically on the continent of Asia had been proven correct, the fate of Korea was not truly critical to American national interests. Even in the event of a "worst case," it was asserted, under circumstances where North Korea, with aid from the PRC or the USSR, unified the Korean peninsula by force, the impact upon Asia—and upon the United States— would be minimal. The Sino-Soviet conflict would remain in one form or another, guaranteeing that the great fault-line providing Asia with a strategic balance would continue to exist. Japan, committed to a policy of separating economics and politics, would adjust to the new circumstances, underwriting an industrial revolution for yet another communist state. Even the United States, finally reconciled to a policy of differentiated interaction with various communist systems, would find it possible to establish a meaningful relation with "the new Korea," as it was likely to have done with "the new Vietnam."

Such theses have been especially attractive to those who are basically committed to a policy of reliance upon communist nationalism to provide Asia—and the world—with a strategic equilibrium, thereby reducing American costs and risks. Yet, from the standpoint of those questioning the type of strategy involved in a unilateral American troop withdrawal from Korea, the theses contain one overriding danger that cannot be ignored or minimized. The most critical issues, including those of peace or war, would become progressively less susceptible to determination, or even initiatives from non-communist sources.

Rival coalitions or configurations would not disappear from the political arena, but to the extent that communist participation was crucial to any such coalition, to the degree that an integral unity or non-communist forces had been rendered impossible, the latter states would be placed in a reactive, defensive posture, operating either as isolated units or as a part of a pure "balance of power" cluster devoid of other cohesive values or policies. One does not have to be an advocate of a return to the cold war to suggest that such a development would ultimately be profoundly destabilizing, quite apart from its impact upon liberal values. Defensiveness would inevitably lead to apprehensions, ultimately to the policies of a garrison state. Extensive dependency upon intra-communist relations, moreover, would heighten the transfer of initiatives to communist states and groups while lending itself to the progressive fragmentation of non-communist states. The capacity of the latter to exercise an independent influence via a combination of forces primarily resting upon non-communist strength and values would have been dissipated.

To make this point is not to argue that a non-communist coalition should necessarily exclude *all* communist states from participation in one form or another. The issue at stake is the ultimate locus of power and authority, hence of values, mode of operations, and sense of responsibility. In sum, at this point in the evolution of global politics, a coalition increasingly dependent upon communist states would be one singularly weak in non-communist cohesion or capacity for decision-making.

The needs of the present run in other directions, it is argued. In an era of protracted, intensive negotiations, those parties are likely to fare best who have the greatest control over the forces clustered under their banners, and who are able to advance initiatives at the appropriate time or to stand firm when that is judged to be proper while, at the same time, avoiding a cumulative series of unilateral concessions. This will be possible only when care is taken to build coalitions of politically and strategically compatible forces.

We have presented this strategic debate in a pure form, one rarely if ever articulated in precisely the manner set forth here. In reality, both sides would accept, indeed, welcome a mix. Those who are prepared to go farthest in accommodating to communist nationalism are willing to acknowledge the importance of certain non-communist ties of a strategic as well as of an economic and political nature. Those who want to focus on strengthening the non-communist forces, making of them as unified and cohesive a force as possible—and one with a clear preponderance of authority within any coalition created —do not reject the idea of utilizing communist divisions. They accept negotiations with communist states, and even agreements that involve alignment for certain purposes. The difference is one of degree, but this makes the fundamental issue none the less important.

Whatever one's judgment concerning this broad strategic debate, the most serious questions to be raised concerning American troop withdrawal from Korea are connected with the timing chosen and the policies that accompanied, or failed to accompany the announcement of a withdrawal time-table. Granting that a case could be made for ground troop withdrawal at some point, and under certain circumstances, the timing and method of executing this policy engendered responses from diverse quarters harmful to the cause of peace and security in the region, and contrary to basic American goals.

At the beginning of the Carter administration, most Asians of whatever political persuasion operated under the shadow of the American abandonment of Vietnam with a strong feeling that the United States was a declining power, a nation lacking the will or capacity to maintain a strategic presence in this part of the world. In its opening actions, moreover, the administration appeared willing to place a priority upon improved relations with Asian communist states against improved relations with erstwhile allies. The rush to Paris to negotiate with the Vietnamese communists, and even the suggestion that aid in some form might be considered caused the American Congress itself to respond sharply in a negative fashion. The enthusiastic pronouncements about the future of the U.S.-PRC relations contrasted with the seeming listlessness in the face of the deteriorating relations with Japan, South Korea, Taiwan, and the Philippines. Without seeking to place the precise balance of blame for these latter developments (it did not rest wholly with the United States), a most confusing picture for Asians now emerged. What *were* American intentions and capacities?

To compound doubts, the American withdrawal pronouncement was made unconditionally. It thus seemed to extend the policy of unilateralism whereby important concessions were made without any *quid pro quo* being advanced. If the North Koreans were as desirous of an American troop withdrawal as their organs indicated, would it not have been wise to hinge that withdrawal to some concrete pledges on the part of P'yŏngyang? Was this not also an opportunity to probe more deeply the willingness of the two major communist states to work toward a peaceful settlement of the Korean issue? At a time when unilateralism was being proffered as a possible American policy on the China front, Korea seemed to fall into a pattern—one profoundly disconcerting to those associated with the United States.[1]

Fortunately, the Carter administration quickly realized that its initial Korean policies had produced unhealthy repercussions, and corrective measures were undertaken. To assuage the fears expressed both in Korea and in Japan, the President reiterated in forceful terms the American commitment to defend South Korea against aggression. If the words of an American leader could deter, the North Koreans had been given an unequivocal warning. Joint American-Korean military exercises seeking to demonstrate the earnestness and effectiveness of an American response were also undertaken. At a later point, moreover, Secretary of Defense Brown and other American spokesmen sought to allay the more general concern regarding a possible strategical withdrawal from the Pacific-Asian region (Brown, 1978). Their statements indicated that while mobility and new weapons systems would take priority over manpower and fixed bases, the United States intended to remain an Asian power. Down to the present these assurances have subsequently been repeated on numerous occasions.

In addition, the Carter administration stood by its commitments with respect to aid in the program of South Korean military modernization, and the Congress approved security assistance of $1,167 million for the fiscal year 1978-1979. In late 1978, moreover, Ambassador William Gleysteen and other American officials assured the Koreans that if American assumptions about Korea's self-defense capacities or the extent of the danger faced proved wrong, current plans would be readjusted (*Korea Herald,* 1978).

By the beginning of 1979, therefore, American credibility with respect to Korea had been partially reestablished, at least for the immediate future. Whether it was necessary to threaten that credibility in the first place, however, is doubtful, and the uncertainties with respect to the middle and long range remain, uncertainties that could reduce the quotient of trust and confidence below that desirable in relations between allies.

II. HUMAN RIGHTS
AND U.S.-ROK RELATIONS

Meanwhile, another issue emerged to render more compli-
cated the American-Korean relationship, that of human
rights. Pak Chŏng-hi was the first thoroughly Asian leader to
hold supreme power in South Korea. Unlike his predecessors,
Pak possessed neither a Western education nor the legacy of a
Judeo-Christian upbringing. His ideals were drawn from the
Meiji Restoration, not from nineteenth century Western
liberalism. His primary goal was to build a strong and prosper-
ous state, one capable of surviving in the treacherous environment of northeast Asia. For him, Confucian values, modified
to be of service in the late twentieth century, and unity—above
all, unity—provided the only feasible route.

As long as the American presence, both in Korea and in
Asia, seemed assured, Pak could be persuaded to experiment
with political liberalization, although it fitted neither his per-
sonality nor his sense of Korea's needs. It must also be asserted
that Pak was far from standing alone. A significant number of
Koreans from every generational group put economic development ahead of political liberalism, strength ahead of democratic attributes in leadership.[2] In 1971, at a point when the
American commitment in Asia seemed increasingly dubious, a
closely contested presidential election took place in Korea.
Foreign policies, especially South-North relations, as well as
domestic issues were featured in public debate. Pak won re-

election by a relatively slim margin, and his opponent, Kim Tae-jung, continued the campaign after the election, going abroad to solicit overseas support, particularly in the United States and Japan. Nothing could have been calculated to concern the Seoul government more, given the importance of American and Japanese assistance and understanding.

Following the Presidential elections, moreover, other events produced cumulative pressures upon the fragile democratic order. The opposition made substantial gains in the National Assembly elections, going over the one-third mark for the first time since 1958. Potentially at least, a succession issue also loomed ahead. Would political division and acrimony increasingly cripple South Korea as Pak's term came to a close in 1975?

In a troubled international environment and with South-North relations taking a new turn, political stability became the chief desiderata for the Republic of Korea government. It was precisely these two factors that Pak was to cite in declaring martial law in the fall of 1972. The United States, South Korea's chief reliance, appeared enroute to withdrawal and defeat in Indochina, and a new chapter in U.S.-China relations was opening, one with uncertain ramifications for the Korean peninsula. By mid-1972, moreover, a dialogue with North Korea had commenced, with the path promising to be long and tortuous.

In the North, an iron-clad unity seemed likely to continue as long as Kim Il-šong lived. Kim had eliminated his opponents within the Korean Workers Party decades earlier, and suppressed all individuals and organizations not in complete conformity with his views. The Democratic People's Republic of Korea (DPRK) represented a throw-back to Stalin-type dictatorship. Yet while demanding that its people speak with one voice, the North Korean leadership sought to advance and utilize differences within the South Korean polity. Kim championed free speech, freedom of assemblage, and other liberal doctrines—as long as they were applicable to South Korea only. Indeed, as we shall later note, the reunification program pushed by

P'yŏngyang's spokesmen rested upon the strategy of combining a monolithic North and a pluralistic South in such a manner as to insure communist victory.

The knowledge of these facts added impetus to the commitment of the South Korean leadership to a dominant party system, one providing a maximum of stability and continuity. No doubt this commitment was strengthened not merely by Pak's deep respect for the accomplishments of the Japanese Meiji Restoration leaders, but also by the fact that contemporary trends elsewhere in Asia were running against Western-style democracy, including the Philippines, another society where American influence had earlier been extensive.

Suddenly, the Pak government moved in an authoritarian direction. On October 17, 1972, slightly over 3 months after the July 4th South-North joint communique signaling the beginning of discussions, President Pak declared martial law, dissolving the National Assembly and suspending portions of the Constitution. Shortly thereafter, a new constitution known as the Yushin (Revitalization) Constitution was drafted and overwhelmingly approved in a national referendum held under martial law in November 1972. Under its provisions, the president is elected by an indirect process making it exceedingly difficult to defeat the incumbent, and presidential powers are greatly expanded in comparison with the previous constitution. Membership in the National Assembly—a body now reduced in authority—is only partly elective, with one-third of its members nominated by the president.

The major opposition party to the Democratic Republican Party (the government party), namely, the New Democratic Party, continued to operate under the Yushin Constitution, and won a sizable number of seats in the National Assembly elections of February 1973.[3] A few months later, in August, Kim Tae-jung was kidnapped in Tokyo by Korean Central Intelligence agents, subsequently to reappear in Seoul, alive as a result of foreign intervention, but placed under indictment. The uproar over the Kim kidnapping led to a rising number of demonstrations and protests, focused chiefly against the Yushin Constitution, spearheaded by students and intellectuals, with a certain number of prominent Christians also involved. At first, the government attempted measures of conciliation, but when these failed, a series of emergency decrees were promulgated in early 1974, combining economic relief for low income groups with stern restrictions upon political freedom. To discuss, propose, or advocate constitutional revision was made punishable by imprisonment up to 15 years, and student political activities were proscribed.

In accordance with these and other regulations, actions were taken in the next several years against political and religious figures who defied the new order as well as against various student and intellectual dissidents.[4] The most widely publicized episode involved the deliberate violation of the existing emergency decrees by a group of liberals on March 1, 1976 when they gathered at Seoul's Myong Dong Catholic Cathedral to call for the restoration of a democratic constitution. This event was staged with the international, and particularly the American audience in mind. The ROK government nevertheless proceeded to arrest, prosecute, and convict those involved, including Kim Tae-jung.

Meanwhile, a relatively unknown candidate for the American presidency had earlier been searching for popular issues. Human rights came naturally to Jimmy Carter given his deeply religious background, but he must also have instinctively recognized its political potential. Soon, moreover, it was seen as a possible means of rebuilding an American consensus on foreign policy. The absence of an ideological component in American foreign policy after the end of monolithic communism had contributed mightily to the breakdown of that consensus. The demand that the risks and sacrifices entailed in American global commitments be supported by moral principles, not merely "balance of power" considerations, was deeply engrained in American tradition. Flying a banner emblazoned with the cause of human rights, could not the president once more mobilize American public support for an activist foreign policy?

The Carter administration thus launched its human rights campaign with great fervor. Abetted by a media that exaggerates every new trend, the human rights crusade appeared to sweep all before it, serving as the test to which each set of bilateral relations would be put. Immediately, apprehensions mounted in Asia from diverse quarters. The quasi-authoritarian states, from Indonesia to South Korea, denounced American criticisms as a new form of cultural imperialism, an attempt to impose foreign values upon them. Privately, they also complained bitterly that attacks were focused upon a select number of countries, many of them historically aligned with the United States, facing complex security problems, and being paragons of virtue in comparison with such states as Cambodia, Vietnam, North Korea, and China—concerning whom official America was almost completely silent. The communist states either ignored the human rights issue completely, or as in the case of the People's Republic of China, contemptuously dismissed it as "a capitalist problem," not applicable to them. The one fully democratic nation of East Asia, Japan, accustomed to separating economics and politics, nervously watched, fearing that the new crusade would do more harm than good.

Predictably, human rights was quickly politicized within the United States, both in governmental policies and within the larger political community. Fortified by the Helsinki Accord, the Carter administration launched its sternest campaign against the Soviet Union, an action ironic in the sense that the USSR had progressed to the point of public trials and a relatively limited number of political prisoners in comparison with the hundreds of thousands of such individuals in camps, prisons, or under surveillance in China and Vietnam, with governmental actions there taken largely in secret, no media coverage being allowed. Yet Washington refrained from pushing the issue on these fronts, appearing to fear that it might jeopardize future relations. Meanwhile, "liberals" and the "left" focused their attention on such governments as those of South Korea, Chile, Iran, South Africa, and similar states while "conservatives" and the "right" tried to call attention to violations in the communist states, new and old.

In truth, there was never any possibility that human rights, however legitimate as a democratic concern, could be the sole or even the primary consideration in formulating American foreign policy. Issues of global strategy and security were certain to figure prominently into such policies, in Washington as in other capitals. Shortly, the Carter administration acknowledged that fact, much to the consternation of some Americans.

From the very beginning, Korea figured prominently in all aspects of the human rights controversy. During the 1976 presidential campaign, certain individuals associated with the Carter candidacy implied that future U.S.-Korean relations would hinge in very considerable measure upon whether the Pak government showed a willingness to undertake political liberalization. The specific issue came to focus upon the imprisonment of the Myong Dong Cathedral group. After Carter's election, American policy began to follow two tracks. On the one hand, private talks between American officials and the Korean government on the subject of human rights continued, with the former urging a liberalization of policies both to improve the general climate of relations and to avert congressional punishment. The latter argument acquired additional validity as a result of "Koreagate," another issue shortly to be discussed. On the other hand, the American government continued to assert publicly that the maintenance of its commitments to Korea, being vital to the stability of northeast Asia, and particularly to Japan, was strongly in the national interest of the United States, and required some modification of the priorities placed upon human rights.

American pressure came from private as well as official sources, ranging from church groups to individuals with a special interest in Korea. Some critics were implacably hostile, indicating that they would be satisfied with nothing short of an overthrow of the Pak government. Others wanted to see reform, not revolution, and an improvement in on-going U.S.-

ROK relations. The former generally vented their attacks in as public a manner as possible. The latter not infrequently outlined their views in private discussions with South Korean authorities.

Undoubtedly, these pressures had some influence, especially those coming via official channels. The ROK government urgently wanted an improvement in over-all American-Korean relations, and at a later point, specifically hoped for a visit from President Carter in connection with his 1979 Asian trip. Thus, most liberal Korean critics were given suspended sentences or released from prison well before their sentences had run their full course. Kim Tae-jung, whose near-martyrdom had made him the Pak government's most formidable foe according to some, threatened to be an exception. At one point, however, he was shifted from prison to a hospital for treatment of neuralgia, and in late December 1978, his release was announced as a part of a general amnesty in connection with the inauguration of President Pak for his second six-year term. Among the 4,000 prisoners released, 106 were reported to be violators of emergency decrees like Kim.

In contrast to its recent treatment of liberals, the ROK government remains uniformly stern in its attitude toward communists or those whom it considers pro-communist. From time to time, small communist cells operating under instructions from P'yŏngyang are uncovered. Those involved can expect no leniency. South Korean poet Kim Chi-ha, some of whose writings showed a pronounced sympathy with pro-communist and communist groups, was initially given a life sentence, later commuted to 20 years.

For all except the infinitesimally small circle of South Koreans sympathetic to, or involved with the DPRK-controlled communist movement, politics in the Republic of Korea remains a complex, constantly shifting contest despite the continuance of the authoritarian cast established in the early 1970s. The New Democratic Party, itself split into "moderate" and "militant" wings, criticizes the government constantly, primarily on domestic issues ranging from corruption to inflation. In the National Assembly elections of 1979 it actually polled a larger number of votes than did the DRP, primarily because of urban unhappiness over inflation. Meanwhile, Kim Tae-jung together with such dissidents as former President Yun Po-sun and certain Christian pastors have openly defied the emergency decrees, denouncing the Yushin Constitution and forming a new organization to challenge the prevailing political order. The government responded by summoning Kim to the Seoul district prosecutor's office for questioning, and giving him warnings. Student demonstrations have periodically taken place, with the leaders sometimes detained, sometimes not.

The situation thus presents a striking contrast to that operative in North Korea, the capital of which, P'yŏngyang, is a scant 225 miles from Seoul. Kim Il-sŏng's message for 1979 contained one passage conveying the flavor of DPRK politics:

> The political function of the entire people held in celebration of the 30th anniversary of the Republic (August 1978) further increased the political force of our revolution. The political and ideological unity of the whole society based on the *chuch'e* (self-reliance) idea has been consolidated as never before and the popular masses' trust in our Party and the Government of the Republic has deepened beyond measure. Today, all our people deem it an infinite honour and happiness to live and make revolution under the care of the Republic, and have a revolutionary determination to fight to the end for the cause of socialism and communism under the banner of the Republic.

Another excerpt, both authoritative and typical, gives further perspective on North Korean political values. The Korean Workers' Party organ, *Nodong Sinmun (The Workers' News),* recently (1979) carried an editorial asserting:

> The greatness of the unity and cohesion of our revolutionary ranks lies in (the fact) that the whole party and the entire people are rallied rock-firm around the Workers' Party of Korea headed by the respected and beloved leader Comrade Kim Il-sŏng on the basis of the *chuch'e* idea.

While factionalism and differences over policy are probably an important element of North Korean politics at the top, the goals of monolithic unity and unswerving obedience to a single party, and via the party, to a single man, constitute the unalleviated refrain of all DPRK organs. In this system, there is no room for an opposition party, nor even a single dissenting voice. All must follow the party line, and do so vocally, not silently.

These facts raise some complex questions about the degree to which concern over human rights should govern American foreign policy, the appropriate method of correlating this concern with others, and the validity of "single country" judgments measured against American cultural standards and objective circumstances, and lacking in any comparative treatment. The argument of those who would apply American human rights criteria rigorously to South Korea is that the United States bears a major responsibility for the creation and survival of this society, and that American support continues to be vital. Hence, the United States has both leverage and a moral responsibility to see that basic democratic values are upheld.

There can be little doubt that in the case of South Korea, American pressures have had some effect, as earlier indicated. Yet if one is to be honest, it must be admitted that one result of giving the human rights issue prominence has been to inject the United States more deeply into the politics of another nation. South Korean opponents of Pak play as much to an American as to a Korean audience, as is evidenced by their organizational activities in the United States, and their efforts to attract the American media as well as the American Congress. The ROK government also shapes its tactics with one eye on likely American responses, and in some degree, uses human rights as a bargaining instrument, in the same manner as does the U.S. government.

In the case of South Korea, two overarching facts shaping recent political developments cannot be ignored. First, American policies pertaining both to Asia and to Korea after the Vietnam debacle reduced American leverage. Second, this development also rendered South Korea less likely to pursue the liberal path, at least for the time being. The Republic of Korea, it should be emphasized, had never been a liberal democratic society of the Western model. The high tide of liberalism was reached during the shortlived Chang Myŏn government, after the student revolt of 1960. Whether that era was characterized by a burgeoning freedom or a growing anarchy, however, remains a hotly debated question, and in retrospect, Chang Myŏn has been a less appealing figure to Koreans than the more authoritarian Syngman Rhee.[5]

Unquestionably, the elements of authoritarianism, built into Korean culture and sustained by a pattern of economic development that until the last 15 years was meager, were heightened after 1971. Yet the most valid comparison remains that with North Korea. Can there by any doubt as to which system is more repressive and less likely to change via an evolutionary process? No South Korean intellectual is forced to recite the thoughts of Pak Chŏng-hi, nor to repeat in rote fashion the precise formulae of a one-party dictatorship. Censorship of public and printed remarks exists, but private conversations remain relatively unrestricted, the surveillance of individuals is limited, and a surprising variety of international news is published, unlike the situation in the North. Travel within the South is quite free, both for citizens and for foreigners. Above all, the South Korean system affords a pluralism of institutions—religious, economic, and even political—that keeps the potential for greater political openness very much alive, in striking contrast to the North. It is partially because of this that privacy is possible. One is not forced to participate in the pageantry of statism on every occasion—and this is a privilege that can only be fully appreciated when it is lost.

The inability of the American government to fine-tune a human rights policy so as to take account of these and other considerations, its seeming lack of capacity to devise and apply an intricately graduated series of incentives and penalties—universally applied—makes human rights both less effective and less moral as a policy than its adherents would like to believe.

Further anomalies are illustrated by the activities of the House of Representatives Subcommittee on International Organizations and Movements. Sustained hearings were held on human rights in South Korea, and subsequently the inquiry was broadened to cover a range of purported Korean efforts to influence American thinking on American-Korean relations. The latter hearings, backed by extensive staff investigations, ranged over the activities of the Unification Church, the Korean CIA, and various other organizations.[6]

In contrast to the lengthy hearings on human rights problems in the ROK, with the initial testimony alone totaling 520 printed pages, human rights in the DPRK took only one day, with the testimony amounting to 70 printed pages, and drawn primarily from U.S. government officials—surely ironic in terms of the ratio of repression, South and North. To assert that this is natural given the paucity of information relating to North Korea and the greater American involvement with the South is satisfying neither on ethical nor on political grounds.

Moreover, the chairman of the International Organizations Subcommittee, Congressman Donald Fraser, was a strong exponent of American troop withdrawal from Korea, and this issue became intertwined with the hearings on occasion. Significantly, some of the dissidents whose cause Congressman Fraser championed insisted privately that they did not want their campaign for a restoration of liberalism in Korea confused with the military withdrawal issue. They asserted that they had made it clear to Fraser as well as to others that they strongly opposed any reduction in American military support since much as they disliked certain policies of the Pak government, they disliked the Communists more. Kim Tae-jung himself has strongly opposed troop withdrawal or other actions that might lend encouragement to the DPRK. These facts were lost in the course of the various hearings in Washington.

How shall we summarize the thorny human rights issue as a factor in U.S.-ROK relations, and on a wider front as well?

An American concern about human freedom is legitimate, and it will continue to find voice in U.S. foreign policy. Moreover, American insistence that political rights be given greater recognition by the ROK government has been of benefit to certain politically active South Korean liberals. Yet the hazards involved in the current application of human rights to American foreign policy are great and must be recognized. The use of this issue for special interests, political and ideological, has been extensive in the United States as elsewhere. The inability or unwillingness, moreover, to establish universally applicable standards or measurements whereby one state can be differentiated from another ensures inequities. These are further enhanced when other considerations governing foreign policy are applied. Surely it is ironic that our pressures come down heavily on states like South Korea, lightly on such states as North Korea and the People's Republic of China.

At this time, our political culture—and that of liberalism in general—cannot be transferred easily or completely to societies bearing a different cultural heritage and facing different contemporary challenges. Indeed, even in the advanced industrial world, democracy faces new and serious problems. We must accept the choices that are available, and in the so-called Third World, these are well exemplified by South and North Korea. To be unable to distinguish between the present status and evolutionary potential of these two societies is both foolish and dangerous. And it is unfortunate yet true that as long as North Korea maintains a monolithic structure, with the mobilized masses subject to the directives of a single man, it will be less easy to move away from authoritarianism in the South. It seems certain, for example, that any government in power in South Korea will demand a high degree of conformity on matters of foreign policy, and especially on the issues of reunification, so as not to present the enemy with a situation that he can employ to his advantage. In its times of greatest peril, the United States did likewise.

III. "KOREAGATE"—AN ASSESSMENT

Another issue that emerged to trouble American-Korean relations in the 1970s was the revelation of Korean government-inspired efforts to purchase American support. Since this issue has seemingly been laid to rest judicially in the United States, perhaps some analysis is possible. There can be no doubt that as the Vietnam disaster loomed ahead, the Korean government acted in panic and often foolishly in an effort to shore up its position in that nation regarded as crucial to its future. It appears that as early as 1970, high-level governmental meetings were held in Seoul to discuss ways whereby U.S. support for South Korea could be sustained. These meetings took on a note of urgency because of the conviction of most South Korean leaders, including President Pak, that the United States was moving toward defeat in Indochina and a radical reappraisal of its Asian commitments.

Elaborate plans were laid to reach various elements in American society. Attention was naturally directed primarily at Congress, but some individuals and groups outside of officialdom were also signaled as being of potential importance, including scholars. Profits from rice sales fueled a goodly portion of the efforts directed toward Congress via the person of Pak Tong-son, the Korean rice dealer. Pak has denied that his actions were directed by the ROK government, but it is highly improbable that his wide-spread political contacts and extensive distribution of "gifts" lay outside the knowledge and approval of Seoul. Moreover, the charges against Kim Dong-jo, former Korean ambassador to Washington, involved direct bribery, and while unprovable, cast a deep shadow over the Korean government's activities during this period, especially since testimony indicated the extensive involvement of the KCIA.

Insufficient attention has been paid to two factors in connection with the Koreagate scandal: the ease with which practices commonplace in societies like Korea and Japan could be transferred to the United States; and the relative lack of sophistication of the Korean government in these matters. Influence peddling by means of various favors, gifts, and grants is a widespread practice by foreign governments and their representatives in the United States as well as within the American community itself. The Korean activities may have been more direct and hence, more clearly illegal as well as unethical, but it would take a massive inquiry with potentially explosive repercussions to indicate the extent to which they deviated from other contemporary operations. In this instance, to be sure, as in others, those Americans who were available for corruption were corrupted, as will always be the case.

Thus, there was some reason for the substantial feeling in Korea that they were being singled out for harsh, prolonged, and exclusive treatment because their nation was small, still heavily dependent upon American support, and hence a convenient target, especially for those who were instinctively against them. Frequently, in private, a bitterness poured out that will not soon disappear. On occasion, it seemed highly irrational to the American observer, or at least, lacking in balance—but the depth of feeling could not be missed. The American policy-maker and the scholar as well are usually reluctant to deal with the realm of sentiment and emotion—since they are impossible to measure and intensely culture-laden. Yet, they play a much greater role in the policies of many nations that we have been willing to admit, and that is certainly true with respect to Asia. Feelings of "sincerity," respect, obligation—concern over "face," proprieties, and responsibility—these are often the essence of the political culture of a nation like Korea, and the lamentable insensitivity of many Americans to these factors has exacted a substantial cost.

It remains an open question as to how seriously the psychological-emotional underpinnings of the American-Korean relation have been bruised, but it would be a great mistake to think that this is a problem confined to Korean officialdom alone. While it is true that in the event of "oppositionists" coming to power, state-to-state relations might operate *de nove*, these same considerations would quickly come into play, as in the past.

The controversy over the testimony of ex-Ambassador Kim Dong-jo provides one example. Understandably, the congressional pressure to make Kim testify under oath was very strong since the integrity of Congress itself appeared to be at stake. At the same time, the State Department could hardly support such a course. The American government, as a matter of policy, would never allow one of its officials to be caused to testify involuntarily under oath in a foreign setting. Indeed, in the Lockheed scandal the American government had gone to considerable lengths to protect the rights even of its private citizens with respect to Japanese proceedings. It should not be surprising, therefore, that as the pressure mounted to make Kim testify, and various retaliatory measures were employed when the Korean government tried to stand firm, a lack of respect for Korean sovereignty was charged. We are not the fifty-first state, one Korean legislator angrily asserted. This issue was finally compromised, with Kim resigning his official post and submitting his answers to questions in writing, but bad feelings remained on both sides.

Koreagate had a strangely anti-climatic, and to many Americans, unsatisfactory end. Several ex-congressmen were found guilty of crimes related to the acceptance of Korean money; a few others were reprimanded for ethically questionable practices, but no sitting congressman was charged with illegal actions. The most celebrated political figure involved, moreover, ex-Congressman Otto Passman, was found innocent by a jury in his home state despite the incriminating testimony of Pak Tong-son who had been given immunity in exchange for his pledge to return to the United States and testify in the Passman trial. Meanwhile, scandals relating to payments from American business to Japanese political leaders mushroomed, with charges against Grumann added to those involving Lockheed, and with evidence indicating that representatives of the U.S. government knew of such practices even if they neither directed nor necessarily condoned them.

An important difference between the Japan scandals and Koreagate does exist in that the latter incident appears to have had extensive government involvement and direction from the beginning. The evidence is now ample, however, that at points in the past, the American government has acted in similar fashion in those situations abroad where it felt its national interests to be threatened, often with the CIA playing a key role. There is no point in trying to determine the complex moral and political issues involved in such activities, especially since each case requires the evaluation of different factors. Suffice it to say that Koreagate has begun to fade into the background since 1978, with both sides hopefully having learned some lessons.

IV. LOOKING AHEAD

Thus far, we have looked primarily at the past. Now it is appropriate to explore the present and future. This requires that we take careful note of the changes that are taking place both in South Korea and in the United States, some of which are scheduled to have a profound influence upon our mutual relations in the years ahead. Looking at Korea first, one sees a society undergoing an extraordinarily rapid transition from backwardness to the status of a relatively advanced, increasingly industrial state. The Republic of Korea today is not a Third World nation as that term is commonly used. Nor is it a minor power, whatever measurement of power be used. In every sense, South Korea is a medium power, and it is still moving upward at a rapid pace. Its economic reach is now global, and of growing importance to such regions as the Middle East and Southeast Asia, not to mention the United States. Its military strength exceeds that of Japan, and in fighting capacity, its land forces may well be equal to those of any other Asian nation, including China, despite the disparity of numbers.

Neither American attitudes nor American policies have kept up with these developments. There is still the tendency to think of Korea as a client state and one serving as an appendage to our Japan policy. In one respect, to be sure, dependency continues in some degree, namely, in the strategic realm. That is also the case with respect to Japan. In all other fields, however, the movement is toward self-reliance and mutuality, and in the military realm as well that is the general thrust.

At this time, American-Korean relations must be regarded as of great importance in their own right. Our economic relations with the ROK have reached major proportions. Cultural relations also enrich the lives of both peoples. Thousands of young Koreans have received their higher education in the United States, and in such fields as the social sciences, intellectual interchange is greater than that between the United States and Japan. A major Korean art exhibition, "Five Thousand Years of Korean Art," came to America in 1979, brilliant testimony to the great cultural traditions of the Korean people. And hundreds of thousands of Americans have come to appreciate many things Korean, from the dance to the cuisine. In Korea, American dress, literature, motion pictures, and art have had a phenomenal vogue.

In the strategic realm also, each party is important to the other. The independence of South Korea and its ability to defend itself against external attack are essential not merely to Japan, but to the political and military equilibrium of East Asia as a whole, and hence to the United States as a Pacific-Asian power vitally affected by developments in this region. Conversely, the continued strategic presence of the United States in Asia, and the credibility of its commitments are of critical significance to South Korea along with many other nations of the area.

For these reasons, current trends in the United States continue to be worrisome to many Koreans, a concern shared with other Asians. A nation still regarded as the most powerful in the world and once viewed as a reliable shield against aggression now appears divided and distracted by its internal problems and uncertain in its international commitments. Some adjustment in the American global role of the 1940s and 1950s was inevitable. The very success of American economic and military assistance rendered key allies progressively stronger, more capable of independence and burden-sharing. As European dominance faded away and a myriad of new states emerged, moreover, the world became increasingly complex, less susceptible to unilateral American influence. The advance of the USSR toward military parity with the United States together with its determination to be recognized as a global power provided an additional complication. In sum, the uses of American power in its various forms were vulnerable to greater limitations and risks. At the same time, the steeply unbalanced character of post-1945 relations between the United States and nations aligned with it was undergoing a change in the direction of greater mutuality, a trend in keeping with the growing capacities of the latter nations.

Defeat in Vietnam, however, disrupted what might have been an orderly adjustment, incremental in nature. After the trauma of Indochina, a sizable number of Americans opted for a widespread and rapid strategic withdrawal, their mood reflective of those traditional American attitudes and policies that had dominated the nineteenth and early twentieth centuries. The focus was upon Asia, but spokesmen for a withdrawal from Europe as well were not lacking. When the early foreign policies of the Carter administration seemed to support the popular mood, at least with respect to the Pacific-Asian region, many Asian governments expressed alarm, even that of the PRC which had come recently to depend upon the United States as a countervailing power to the Soviet Union. That the world's most powerful nation should suddenly appear vacillating and unpredictable was destabilizing.

When the Carter administration discovered the repercussions of its early policies, changes were made, as previously noted. An effort was mounted to stem the tide of strategic withdrawal from Asia, to reassert America's stake in, and commitment to a strategic balance in Pacific-Asian region. Controversy shifted, to center upon the question of a united front versus an equilibrium strategy. United front advocates supported the concept of an informal alignment of the United States, Japan, and China to confront the Soviet Union in Asia, arguing that there was no other way to halt Russian expansion, and that such expansion—coupled with Soviet operations elsewhere—represented a direct threat to the American national interest. Those favoring an equilibrium strategy maintained that the United States should seek a rough balance in its relations with Russia and China, accepting the fact that these relations would be different since the USSR was a global power, China at most a regional force at present. They opposed any sustained tilt toward either major communist state, asserting that the United States should negotiate from strength on an issue by issue basis with both states, with U.S. interests and those of our close allies constantly kept in mind. To them the united front strategy had two fatal defects: first, it would make crucial negotiations with the Soviet Union on issues vital to the survival of all increasingly difficult, if not impossible; second, it would be destabilizing for Asia, since China's own expansionist inclinations, especially toward Southeast Asia, would be strengthened.

The Carter administration finally pronounced itself officially as committed to an equilibrium strategy, but there was evidence of continuing differences of opinion within the government, not infrequently reflected in policy. Meanwhile, however, despite official disavowal, withdrawal remained a factor with which to conjure, primarily because grass-roots support among the American citizenry at large for internationalist policies—economic, political, and strategic— remained uncertain and subject to severe strains.

Concern over domestic problems continues to mount in the United States. Inflation currently dominates the list of issues, but the related problems of energy shortages, quality education, progressive bureaucratization—non-governmental as well as governmental—the frustrations of urban life, and the heightened competition for "desirable" occupations all bear down upon the average American. With most Americans having reached an unprecedented pinnacle of affluence, the citizen is now asked to reconstruct a life-style in the direction of conservation and austerity. Unquestionably, this is required, and there is much waste to be eliminated, but it remains an audacious request, politically hazardous to those in authority, especially since a sizable segment of the population still considers itself on the lower rungs of affluence and upwardly mobile. The structural changes required of the American economy are no less fundamental, and will be no less difficult to achieve.

The United States is thus entering uncharted waters. Its strength—actual and potential—remains enormous. Yet, factors of leadership and policy will combine to determine the degree to which that strength can be mobilized and toward what ends it will be directed. In any case, it seems certain that the tackling of America's domestic problems will assume the highest priority for the foreseeable future. This does not mean an abandonment of international involvement. The U.S. economic and political stake in a stable, peaceful world, one capable of constructive interaction, has never been greater. There are dangers on the horizon, however, that should not be minimized. For example, the support for economic "protectionism" has not been stronger since the 1930s, with approval emanating from both business and labor. In any case, the forms which American foreign policy takes in the final decades of the twentieth century are certain to be derived from the trends that prevail on the domestic front, specifically, the results of the campaign now in its opening stages to restructure American society.

It should not be thought that the United States stands alone in facing the problems sketched here so briefly. It moves in company with other advanced industrial societies, none of which are without similar difficulties, albeit, with variations in intensity. The Soviet Union, moreover, confronts at least equally grave problems as it struggles to catch up with the advanced nations. Despite repeated attempts at reform, the Soviet system nurtures bureaucratism, dampens initiatives, and protects mediocrity. These defects have not prevented economic growth, to be sure, nor the advent of ever greater military strength. Yet with these, and a growing Russian involvement in the world, have come the beginnings of more complex fissures within Soviet society, including the desire of the Soviet people for living standards comparable to those of the affluent societies and a greater measure of political/cultural openness. Will not these developments increasingly serve as constraints upon Soviet expansionism in the coming decades?

We speak today of "balance of power" policies as dominating international relations. In reality, we are moving toward a balance of weakness insofar as the major societies are concerned, a balance all the more paradoxical because of the level to which military armaments have been raised. These conditions are likely to put a premium upon regionalism in the future, and enhance the authority, as well as the responsibility, of the medium powers of the world. The commitments of the United States in two regions, namely, Western Europe and East Asia, are likely to remain substantial due to the nature of American interests, but progressively, the premium will be upon reciprocity, a sharing of obligations.

V. U.S.-ROK ECONOMIC RELATIONS

If this represents aspects of the American scene, how do we assess trends with respect to the Republic of Korea? The year 1977 marked the launching of South Korea's fourth Five-Year Economic Development Plan. In the 15 years since 1963, the Republic of Korea has achieved an annual average GNP growth rate of more than 10 percent, making it one of the most rapidly developing societies in the world. This is all the more remarkable because the earlier picture was so unpromising. American economic aid was crucial to the survival of South Korea in its initial years,[7] but war and political instability interwoven with indecision or conflict over economic policies rendered development negligible. Many observers were prepared to write South Korea off as a hopeless case. In those years, the economic accomplishments of North Korea were considerably more auspicious.

Starting in the early 1960s, however, the situation changed. The military government established in 1961 brought about political stability while, at the same time, giving economic development the highest priority. Professionals and technicians from the civilian sector were recruited and given ample authority to develop comprehensive economic plans. A new governmental relationship was established with business, combining encouragement and direction. Essentially, the model adopted was that of Japan, with a very heavy premium upon export expansion, especially to the more advanced economies. The results are well known. In 1978, Korean per capita annual income reached $1,242, with the figure for 1979, $1,550. Measured against the standards of the region, moreover, income distribution is reasonably good. Among the eight non-communist developing nations of East and South Asia, Korea's income equality is exceeded only by that of Taiwan. Particularly noteworthy is the fact that by 1977, the average farm family income stood at $2,960, slightly higher than that of the average urban family's yearly receipts ($2,903), indicating that the historic urban-rural gap had been remedied to a significant extent.

Gross National Product shot up 12.5 percent in 1978, reaching $46 billion in current prices, and seems likely to advance rapidly in 1979 despite governmental efforts to dampen the boom by keeping growth to 8 percent. Unemployment is at its lowest level in years, being slightly over 3 percent. Foreign trade reached a phenomenal $27.2 billion in 1978 (compared to $55 million in 1962), with an additional spurt to $34 billion in 1979. Income from services, notably construction and related projects in the Middle East, shipping, and tourism, provided an additional $5.8 billion.

What has accounted for these striking gains? Among many factors, perhaps two warrant emphasis. First, South Korea belongs to that group of societies partaking of a Sinic culture, and thus tradition has loaned assistance in at least three crucial respects: respect for education, experience in complex organization, and commitment to a work ethic. Together with such societies as Japan, Taiwan, Hong Kong, and Singapore, the Republic of Korea has demonstrated that these assets, when effectively utilized via a stable political system *and* realistic economic policies, can be of inestimable importance.

Second, the South Korean developmental plan was properly constructed and timed to take advantage of the prevailing international environment, especially the opportunities for a growing economic interaction with two of the world's economic giants, the United States and Japan. The ROK plan called initially for extensive borrowing to construct a modern industrial sector as rapidly as possible. Then, by utilizing a literate, increasingly skilled labor force and the relatively low costs of industrial raw materials, South Korea was able to capture a part of the increasing markets for industrial goods of varying types, not only in the United States and Japan, but on an ever broader front, including the newly developing countries. The ROK also moved rapidly toward higher technology production, thereby entering into new fields of competition with the advanced industrial states. As we have indicated, South Korea used the earlier experience of Japan as a its model, and it came to this model in sufficient time to make it work equally well.

One of South Korea's proudest recent accomplishments has been improvement in rural life, and this has occurred through a novel program known as the *Saemaŭl Undong* (New Community Movement). Starting on a very small scale, the Saemaŭl Movement has represented an effort by government to encourage village modernization by primary reliance upon local initiatives, stimulated via economic incentives and political exhortation. In the fall of 1970, having an over-supply of cement, the government provided 335 sacks to every South Korean village. Those villages using their gift effectively were rewarded the following year by being given additional assistance.

From this modest beginning, the Saemaŭl Movement has mushroomed into a massive community development program involving village centers, public baths, irrigation expansion, reforestation, local industries, and a host of other improvements. Governmental costs have been relatively low, with the bulk of the expenses being borne through the proceeds from the projects themselves. Sizable rural credit facilities have been accumulated.

A concentrated program aimed at increasing agricultural productivity—long neglected in South Korea—also got underway after 1972. By means of improved seed strains, price supports, expanded water conservancy, chemicalization and mechanization, grain production increased markedly, exceeding 6 percent in some years. Nevertheless, South Korea remains dependent upon external sources for about one-fourth of its grain needs, obtaining most of this grain from the United States. Despite rural improvements, moreover, the drift toward urbanization has continued. In 1961, nearly 57 percent of the population was rural; by 1978, this figure was only 38 percent.

How do the economic gains of South Korea compare with those of the North Korea, a question that has both political and strategic significance?[8] Up to the mid-1960s, the DPRK surpassed the ROK in both industrial and agricultural growth. In the past decade, however, the South has moved well ahead of the North in overall economic development, and the gap is likely to become larger in the years immediately ahead. The South's industrial production is the key factor, with current increases in the ROK being approximately twice those of the DPRK. In grain production, North Korea's gains probably exceed those of the South, taking the past decade as a whole, with chemicalization and mechanization having reached very high levels. The recent advances of the South, however, are bringing it abreast of the North here also, and ROK improvements in general rural livelihood have probably surpassed those of the DPRK in the last 5 years.

What has given South Korea its growing economic edge? Many factors are involved. Labor productivity has increased more rapidly, the result of the priority given to economics and of a much wider contact with the advanced industrial world. Whereas the North has been allocating between 15 and 20 percent of its GNP annually to defense, moreover, the South's commitments have been about 6 percent in the last several years, up from less than 5 percent. In addition, the South has allocated its investment funds much more efficiently as well as acquiring major resources from abroad stemming from its emphasis upon export expansion. The North, on the contrary, was able to generate far too little export earnings, with the result that in its effort to modernize its industrial plant in the early 1970s, it accumulated large foreign debts. Unable to meet the payments, North Korea became the first communist state to default involuntarily on its international obligations. This naturally affected its access to advanced technology, and together with heavy defense expenditures and adverse weather, caused the Six-Year Plan (1971-1976) industrial targets to be missed.

It is anticipated that the DPRK growth rate in the next 5 years will probably be 6 percent at a maximum, whereas the South is likely to continue to grow at 8 to 9 percent barring some major catastrophe, making the Southern economy about three times the size of that in the North, although the ROK population is only about twice that of the DPRK (CIA, 1978). If this proves to be true, it will increase pressures upon North Korea to reach some accommodation with South Korea, unless it elects to risk another military confrontation.

Meanwhile, success has posed its problems as well as its promises for the South. The most serious of the problems has been inflation, a product of an over-heated economy. The inflation rate in 1978 was at least 15 percent, and in 1979, it has been estimated at 25-30 percent. On the surface, the approach to this problem has been somewhat contradictory but over time, it may prove to be sound. On the one hand, the Economic Planning Board has moved to scale down certain major developmental projects in heavy and chemical industries, and to restrain the feverish government drive for exports. Some funds are to be diverted into the light industrial sector of the economy in an effort to increase domestic supplies of consumer goods. At the same time, the economy is being liberalized, with prices allowed to rise, import restrictions reduced, and increased scope given the private sector. The government hopes that these measures will eventually result in a balanced economy, with spending—both governmental and private—lowered, and confidence among producers and consumers in the state's capacity to control inflation reestablished. The danger, of course, as elsewhere in the world, lies in a continued inflationary spiral, or in rising political unrest due to stern economic measures.

On balance, however, prospects for sustained economic advances appear good. Tight credit is likely to be one of the chief constraints upon growth in the years ahead. There are also going to be rising labor costs and problems of securing sufficient managerial talent, factors that may affect the profits of the industrial sector. The goal of maintaining an average annual real growth of 8-9 percent up to 1986, however, is by no means unattainable, assuming an avoidance of a global depression.

How does the South Korean economic picture relate to U.S.-ROK economic relations? First, in scope, U.S. economic relations with South Korea have grown at a pace commensurate with the extraordinary development of the South Korean economy. Some 27 percent of total ROK trade in 1978 was with the United States and approximately one-third of its exports went to this nation (Youngil Lim, 1979). Korean exports to the United States amounted to $4 billion; imports from the United States totalled $3 billion. Private U.S. investment in South Korea has now reached nearly $1 billion, and such investment has been accelerating in recent years. That figure, it might be noted, is considerably less than Japanese private investment. The latter accounts for 59 percent of total foreign investment whereas the investment of private American companies amounts to only 18 percent, concentrated mainly in such large-scale projects as oil refining, automobiles, chemicals, and electronics.

The economic issues between the two nations are similar in type, if less formidable in intensity, to those involving U.S.-Japan economic relations, and stem from the same basic causes. The U.S. trade deficit with the ROK, which reached $1 billion in 1978, while far from the $11 billion deficit with Japan, nonetheless represented a worrisome problem, especially since it seemed likely to persist, probably to grow. As in the case of Japan, quotas are being applied to various Korean manufactures entering the United States in an effort to lessen the impact upon American-made products. The Korean effort, moreover, is toward market diversification, with less dependence upon the United States and Japan. Major portions of the American business community regard such measures as insufficient, however, and protectionist sentiment continues to rise. South Korea, in addition, is buying advanced technology at an accelerated rate from the United States and Japan, promising greater competitiveness in the years ahead.

On the American side, until certain structural changes are effected in the economy as a whole, problems will persist. First, a meaningful energy program must be inaugurated, accompanied by other measures to bring inflation under a greater measure of control. Means also need to be found to assist in the phasing out of obsolescent industries, and in promoting more extensive research and development so that the United States remains on the frontiers of advances in science and technology. Within industry, labor productivity must be improved, and American entrepreneurs must accept the challenge of entering more vigorously into competition for world markets. To abet such a trend, the U.S. government should construct a set of international economic policies consciously designed to forward the U.S. role in the global market-place.

On the Korean side, the need is to reduce the almost exclusive emphasis upon export expansion and double-digit growth rates. Increased attention must be paid to the domestic market, and to internal social services. At the same time, more rapid liberalization should take place, with import and investment barriers removed or reduced, enabling a more balanced and equitable economic relationship.

Certain steps in these directions are underway, and interaction in economic matters between the United States and the ROK has recently been intensified, both at governmental and private sector levels. In the spring of 1979, the ninth meeting between United States and ROK Department of Commerce heads took place, followed in late May by a fourth joint meeting of the U.S.-Korea and Korea-U.S. Economic Councils, associations composed of business leaders of the two societies. Modelled after a similar Japanese group, a 30-member Korean buying mission in the United States negotiated some $2.3 billion in purchasing contracts in early 1979 in an effort to close the trade gap. ROK officials also promised a broad liberalization program while calling upon the United States to harness its capital and technology to Korea's industrious and skilled labor pool.

South Korea will need to borrow as much as $2 billion per annum for the next several years if it is to achieve current economic goals. Meanwhile, the prospects are for a sizable overall trade deficit for the ROK in 1979, much of it with Japan, as in the past. Thus, increased purchases from the United States may constitute a strain. Yet, as Secretary of Commerce Juanita Kreps declared in her 1979 visit to Seoul, the likelihood is strong that South Korea will soon surpass France and Italy to become the seventh most important trading partner of the United States.

The U.S.-ROK economic relationship is thus truly vital. Yet the structural changes outlined earlier cannot come quickly or easily, however essential they may be. In recent years, the United States has slipped into the role historically played by colonial economies. While not without important exports of manufactured products, increasingly, the United States has relied upon exports of agricultural items, including industrial raw materials, and in turn, purchased huge quantities of finished goods from abroad, accumulating ever larger trade deficits. The post-war economic game plan of nations like Japan and Korea, enormously successful up to the present, must now be modified, just as the U.S. economy must be revitalized.

VI. POLITICAL AND SECURITY RELATIONS

Politics in the Republic of Korea are based upon a dominant party system, underwritten by current political institutions and regulations authoritarian in nature, epitomized by the Yushin Constitution and Emergency Decree Number 9. Yet the South Korean political system is also one that sustains social and economic pluralism together with a surprising political diversity. The New Democratic Party, for example, has recently stepped up its opposition to governmental policies. Prior to its national convention of May 30-31, 1979, a spirited campaign took place between Yi Chol-sung (Lee Chul-seung), party head in recent years, and Kim Yong-sam (Kim Young-sam), former leader, with Kim being the victor. In the course of campaigning, Kim indicated that he regarded the NDP under Yi's leadership as anemic in its approach to the ruling DRP, and promised much more vigorous opposition.

Kim Tae-jung used his influence within the NDP to aid Kim Yong-sam, and may have been a decisive factor in the election. Subsequently, both Kim Tae-jung and ex-president Yun Po-sun were appointed NDP advisors, thereby establishing a united front of dissidents likely to prove more militant, especially on domestic issues. Watching such developments closely, DPRK leaders proposed talks with Kim Yong-sam, pursuing an opening presented by Kim himself—but this offer was finally rejected. Differences over tactics and strategy regarding South-North relations may surface, however, and in general, ROK politics are currently more volatile than at any time in the recent past, with the Pak government likely to pursue some combination of policy adjustments to meet NDP challenges and stern control of the opposition when it feels that public order or basic policies are threatened.

At an earlier point, Kim Tae-jung, released from prison in late December, 1978, had immediately announced the formation of a new political group, the People's Alliance for Democracy and National Unification, with its nucleus composed of some of the Myong Dong Cathedral dissidents. Kim, once the NDP leader himself and viewed by the government as the major political threat, has played a cat and mouse game, with governmental authorities responding in kind. Knowing that President Pak did not want to jeopardize the scheduled visit of President Carter in June, Kim repeatedly challenged prevailing regulations, thereby daring the Pak government to arrest him.

In an interview in April 1979 with a *Newsweek* correspondent, for example, Kim denounced the present system as "dictatorial rule," and called for an immediate end to Emergency Decree No. 9 (Kim Dae Jung, 1979). He also asserted that while there had been "brilliant economic growth in recent years," a lack of balance in distributing economic and social justice prevailed, threatening to erode public loyalty. Analogies with South Vietnam and Iran were drawn. In addition, Kim indicated that while he strongly opposed Communism and disagreed with the Carter administration's troop withdrawal policy, "the democratization" of South Korea was essential so that "we can deal with North Korea on a sound basis."

As noted earlier, Kim had been warned previously that his criticisms could subject him to arrest, and on one occasion, he had been taken to police headquarters for questioning. In April, he was again put under house arrest, but contacts with both Koreans and foreigners continued. It is impossible to assess Kim Tae-jung's political strength among the South Korean citizenry at present. He was given a major boost, of course, via the kidnapping incident and his near martyrdm. The issues upon which he is concentrating, however, may be co-opted by Kim Yong-sam, or in some degree, by the government itself. In the 1979 elections, the principal concern of the electorate was clearly the economy, and especially the rapid rise in urban livelihood costs, which had advanced by some 33 percent in the previous year. Economic issues now combine with increased political confrontation to pose growing problems. The government can no longer concentrate upon economic management alone. While it can probably count upon continuing divisions within the opposition, it needs a more appealing political strategy than that of increased suppression if it is to retain popular support. In this scene, the opposition must also bear responsibility for its actions. There is a certain tendency at present for neither side to want to look "weak," yet escalating confrontations could do severe damage to the nation as a whole.

If the New Democratic Party constitutes the legal opposition and the People's Alliance for Democracy and National Unification a quasi-legal opposition, presently in some degree of alignment with NDP, what of the underground communist movement? Every indication suggests that the number of communist adherents in the ROK is minuscule despite repeated efforts by the North to seed and feed underground cells. Periodically, individuals or small groups are uncovered who have been given training, funds, and instruction by Korean Workers' Party representatives. The easiest conduit is the General Confederation of Korean Residents in Japan, long a Tokyo-based, DPRK-controlled organization, but agents have also been transferred directly from North Korea, usually by boat.

Radicalism in South Korea, however, rarely takes the form of an adoration of Kim Il-sŏng and his "state of paradise." The small but not insignificant student-intellectual radical circles within the ROK's major institutions of higher learning have tended to turn to a wide diversity of other heroes and models, ranging from Mao and Che Gueverra to Herbert Marcuse, coming to them via Japanese and Western (chiefly American) sources. In these forms, Marxism of a salon type has had a certain vogue among a few young rebels, along with the doctrines of social democracy. Enthusiasm for the DPRK, however, shows no signs of growing.

Notwithstanding this fact, the Korean Workers' Party conducts its own "Viet Cong" operation, having launched the so-called Revolutionary Party for Reunification (RPR), a purely Northern creation totally loyal to The Great Leader in P'yŏngyang. The RPR purports to operate a clandestine radio station in the South, but in fact, the Voice of the RPR broadcasts from Haeju, close to the ROK border.

In one sense, it is remarkable that a nation with the most limited democratic traditions and one virtually surrounded by communist states, has been able to preserve any significant quotient of political openness. And it is all the more remarkable given the broad trends governing Pacific-Asian international relations in the past decade, including the lessened credibility of the United States. Nor does the priority placed upon rapid economic development necessarily abet the democratic cause, as the experience of many emerging states so eloquently testifies.

Nevertheless, until civil liberties are given greater weight in Korean political life—for example, until it is possible to discuss legally the Yushin Constitution and until individuals like Kim Tae-jung are wholly free—tensions will remain in the American-Korean relationship. Thus, discussion should continue both at official and unofficial levels pertaining to this issue from the American side, indicating the costs of repression and listening to the Korean position, aware of the fact that the United States should not insist that the Korean polity be shaped into a precise replica of the American structure, ignoring the differences in traditions and contemporary circumstances. Under these conditions, serious conversations conducted in private (hence, not for the purpose of enhancing a given individual's or side's public image) have been productive on occasion in the past. In some cases, it should be noted, there are very concrete issues—questions of fact and their implications—at stake. For example, authoritative Korean spokesmen have argued privately that their principal concern in the case of Kim is that if he were given permission to go to the United States or Japan, he would seek to mount a movement representative of a "third Korea," thereby complicating future South-North negotiations. Is this a valid concern or an excuse, and what measures might be discussed to meet the concern if it is determined to be valid?

In the matter of human rights, private organizations can and should often play a more important role than government. Unfortunately, however, some organizations supposedly devoted to human rights are so ideologically or emotionally laden as to sacrifice their credibility. Among these are groups that are willing to accept almost any government to the "left" of the American system, however repressive, and to concentrate upon governments which they label "right." Other organizations, however, such as Freedom House, are engaged in the complex task of seeking to establish criteria for measuring progress and retrogression in human rights on a universal basis.[9] There is always the danger of ethnocentrism in such an undertaking, but in an age when nearly every government proclaims its legitimacy to derive from the support of its citizenry, insists upon calling itself a democracy, and defends its policies as aimed at enhancing the welfare of its people, it is not amiss to inquire into these matters, providing they are put into a universal framework, and providing also that they do not lead to a moral unctuousness, lending itself to a new form of imperialism. Surely it would be ironic if human rights were used as an excuse for the repudiation and abandonment of South Korea, leading to "liberation" of the Hanoi type.

On a more positive note, the time is now ripe for the establishment of an inter-parliamentary discussion group, with participants from the U.S. Congress and the ROK National Assembly. Such a group already connects South Korean and Japanese legislators, and as we have noted, exists between the U.S. and ROK business communities. It should meet regularly, with some rotation of membership, its participants prepared to address those issues that seem most germane to bilateral relations, speaking frankly in off-the-record sessions designed to acquaint each other with the individual and collective views of all parties concerned.

Meanwhile, a substantial change in American policy has taken place with respect to security matters. The Carter administration's initial plan was to withdraw 33,000 American troops from Korea by 1982, together with all of the nuclear weapons within the country. The first phases of this withdrawal took place during 1978. Originally, 6,000 American troops were to be pulled out by the end of the year, but congressional opposition along with the growing realization of the negative impact of the withdrawals upon our Asian allies caused the Carter administration to alter its plans. Only one combat battalion of 800 men and 2,600 noncombatants were actually removed, with an additional 2,600 scheduled to be taken out in 1979. Moreover, U.S. air force strength in Korea was increased, and it was announced that F-15 and F-14 jets would shortly be provided U.S. units there.

Two developments in the latter part of 1978 raised additional questions about the withdrawal program. In late October, the United Nations Command in Korea announced the discovery of yet another North Korean tunnel (two had been uncovered earlier, in November 1974 and March 1975). The newly discovered tunnel was in the southern sector of the DMZ near Panmunjom, less than 30 miles north of Seoul, and it was large enough to enable soldiers to move through it, three to four abreast (Sungjoo Han, 1979). This seemed to represent a convincing rebuttal to those who argued that there was no basis for concern about a possible conflict on the Korean peninsula.

Later, a new U.S. Army intelligence report was prepared, indicating that North Korean military strength was greater than had been previously been estimated. The official report has not been made public, but it is now estimated that the professional DPRK army may contain 41 divisions, with total military manpower exceeding 600,000, possessing more than 2,000 tanks, with combat-ready units extending in depth along the Demilitarized Zone. It had long been known that the North Korean air force greatly outnumbered that of South Korea, although its planes are mainly older MiG-21s.

Using this report as one justification, the Carter administration announced following the President's visit to Korea, on July 20, 1979, that further withdrawal of U.S. ground combat troops "should await credible indication" that a satisfactory military balance with the North had been restored and that "a reduction of tension is underway." Although American authorities continue to pledge ultimate ground troop withdrawal, they have postponed further reductions at least until a reappraisal of the situation in 1981. Meanwhile, President Carter had already obtained from Congress approval for a $1.2 billion military assistance program for the Republic of Korea in August 1978, with additional sales being projected for later periods. The emphasis was particularly upon improving South Korean air and naval capacities. At the same time, South Korean defense industries were being developed at an accelerated pace. In the fall of 1978, medium and longer range ground-to-ground missiles and multiple-loaded rockets developed by Korea were successfully tested (Sungjoo Han, 1979). A new lightweight tank was also being developed.

Coordination in military planning and exercises has recently been significantly advanced. In November 1978, the U.S.-Korea Combined Forces Command was officially activated, with high-ranking South Korean military officers participating in the actual planning and execution of military operations. Some 5 months later, in March 1979, the U.S. and ROK held a 17-day joint military exercise involving 100,000 Korean and 56,000 American personnel. This joint exercise, the fourth of its type, was the largest yet staged in South Korea and involved every kind of unit, with American forces coming from far away as Fort Sill, Oklahoma.

It is possible, though unprovable, that North Korea's agreement to return to a Panmunjom negotiating table with the South in early 1979 was prompted in some measure by the desire to prevent an American reversal of policy on troop withdrawal, together with the hope of bringing the Americans to bilateral discussions. In any case, in this volatile and unpredictable era, the United States should pursue security policies regarding the Republic of Korea which reduce to an absolute minimum the possibility of any communist miscalculation regarding U.S. intentions. Nearly all South Koreans—and a great many other Asians—believe that the surest means of preserving peace on the Korean peninsula is to retain an American military presence. By a military presence, moreover, the Koreans mean some ground forces. In commenting upon the announcement of the scheduled withdrawal of an infantry battalion in December 1978, the executive editor of the *Korea Herald*, a newspaper reflecting government views, voiced the opinion that behind Carter's policies was the desire to prevent any American soldier from being shot—in Korea or elsewhere in Asia—a response reflective of the Vietnam disaster. But, continued the writer, can the U.S. pledge be fulfilled merely by means of air power?... "we doubt that war planes alone can be an effective deterrent against an invasion attempt by the North Koreans. Besides, aircraft can fly away at an instant's notice. And no matter how good the U.S. administration's intentions may be, would the U.S. Congress and American public sanction a return to Korea at the time of crisis once ground troops have been withdrawn? (Korea Newsreview, 1978)."

The current situation, in sum, provides exceedingly strong justification for the suspension of American troop withdrawal from Korea which has taken place. Let us suppose that Kim or his successor continues to refuse to negotiate with the South Korean government on any reasonable basis, rejects all proposals for reciprocal recognition of the two Korean governments by the major powers, refuses to sit in the United Nations with the ROK, continues the attempt to cultivate a revolutionary movement within South Korea, and retains its military forces within hours—or by air, minutes—of Seoul, meanwhile proceeding to build up those forces as well as to continue the hardening of military and industrial sites against aerial attack.

Under these conditions, is it not entirely appropriate for the United States to halt all ground troop withdrawal until North Korea gives some evidence of accepting the status-quo pending a peaceful resolution of the Korean problem?

The Congress has required the administration to report to it on the viability of further withdrawals 120 days before each new phase. Consequently, a venue for a policy change exists, and if the militancy of the North Korean government remains unaltered, is it really possible to say that further American military withdrawals are forwarding peace and stability in the region?

Meanwhile, exercises involving coordinated American ground, air, and sea forces should continue on a regular basis. Spokesmen of the U.S. government, moreover, should remind P'yŏngyang—and others—that in the event of aggression against South Korea, the use of nuclear weapons against the aggressor is not precluded, thereby reiterating an earlier American pledge. Further, security assistance to the ROK should be continued on schedule, with strenuous efforts being met by both parties to see that waste is controlled and effective use made of such aid. At the same time, the Pak administration should be encouraged in its present policies of not raising the ratio of military to civilian development above 30/70. Also, the joint American-Korean security consultative sessions should not only be regularly conducted, but agreement should also be sought at these sessions on all matters pertaining to Korean security, including plans for various contingencies, with appropriate recommendations to the two governments. Finally, the South Korean militia should be strengthened, both for the purpose of bolstering morale and for an in-depth intensive defense.

VII. THE SOUTH-NORTH ISSUE

No examination of U.S.-ROK relations—the current issues and future alternatives—can be complete without probing the question of American policies with respect to the Democratic People's Republic of Korea. A certain body of opinion in the United States argues that we should entertain direct negotiations with the Kim government, first, because the issue of transforming the Korean armistice into a peace settlement involves the United States and North Korea directly, and beyond this, because only through direct negotiations can the United States have any leverage upon North Korean policies, helping to shift the DPRK from isolation and sole dependence upon communist support—hence, moving it gradually away from militancy and intransigence.

When the issues are put in this form, however, the real question is obscured. That question can be put very simply. Should the United States enter into negotiations with North Korea that exclude the participation of South Korea? The objective of the Kim Il-sŏng government—borrowing from the tactics of the Hanoi government at the time of the Geneva peace discussions in the 1970s—remains precisely this. Kim has made it emphatically clear that he wants bilateral discussions with Washington excluding Seoul. Up to the present, at least, he has rejected the idea of trilateral discussions involving the United States together with both South and North Korea. Kim's position has been that bilateral discussions should be pursued with the United States regarding a peace treaty while

North-South bilateral discussions deal with reunification. On both scores, however, Kim has betrayed serious inconsistencies, as we shall see. Regarding the United States, he has on occasion indicated a willingness to discuss many issues, including his One Korea proposals. Toward the ROK, he has recently rejected negotiations with the presently constituted government despite an earlier willingness to do so.

To understand these facts, some background on DPRK policies regarding the South-North issue and the United States is required.[10] South-North Korean discussions first opened at Panmunjom on August 17, 1971 in the context of a dramatically changing international situation. The initial meetings were between Red Cross liaison officers, followed by South-North Red Cross "preliminary meetings," and ultimately, a full South-North Red Cross Conference. Meanwhile, after secret meetings in May involving top-level ROK and DPRK officials, the Joint Communique of July 4, 1972 was made public. To a surprised world, Seoul and P'yŏngyang appeared to have agreed upon three important principles in connection with unification: that it would be achieved through independent Korean efforts, without external imposition or interference; that it would be achieved through peaceful means, not through the use of force against each other; and that a great national unity would be sought, transcending differences in ideas, ideologies, and systems.

It was also agreed that to foster an atmosphere of mutual trust, the two sides would not slander or defame each other, or undertake armed provocations. It was further provided that exchanges in various fields would be promoted, and efforts would be made to conclude the Red Cross talks successfully. A direct telephone line between Seoul and P'yŏngyang was set up to deal with any problems arising, and a South-North Coordinating Committee—co-chaired by Yi Hu-rak, the head of the ROK CIA, and Kim Yŏng-ju, Kim Il-sŏng's brother—was created to give effect to these principles.

Unfortunately, 1972-1973 marked the high point in the dialogue. No progress was made in the talks primarily because of an irreconcilable set of differences in the position of the two sides. South Korea insisted upon a step-by-step program, starting with the humanitarian task of bringing divided families into contact with each other, progressing to economic relations, and—only after these programs were operating successfully—moving forward to the complex task of reconciling political and military policies. North Korea, on the other hand, demanded some dramatic initial steps in the political-military field as an opening stage, including the reduction of the armed forces of each side to an equal number, possibly as low as 100,000, and the creation of a single federated Korea based upon equal representation from North and South.

Other problems were to emerge, however. The military build-up of the North recommenced in 1970, and has not slackened. It has been estimated that DPRK military expenditures in recent years have averaged 15-20 percent of the total GNP, and this increased expenditure commenced well before the recent South Korean buildup began. Nor did support cease for the northern-founded Revolutionary Party for Reunification, to which reference was earlier made. Through the period of negotiations, it continued to launch vitriolic attacks on the ROK government, with DPRK officials pretending that it was an instrument of Southern revolutionaries, hence, not under their control.

In mid-1973, North Korea suspended the full-scale SNCC talks, asserting that the South's anti-communist actions made continuance impossible. In view of the fact that Kim Il-sŏng had accepted the head of the ROK CIA as the South's chief negotiator in 1972, held a friendly conversation with him, and had been well aware of ROK policies regarding communism throughout the entire period, this was an extremely thin excuse. Progressively, other aspects of the dialogue were terminated—all by P'yŏngyang. In May 1975, talks between the two SNCC vice chairmen looking toward resumption of the plenary meetings were boycotted by the North. The direct telephone line was cut off on August 20, 1976, 12 days after the axe murder of two Americans at Panmunjom. Finally, the "working level" Red Cross talks—which had been purely nominal—were canceled indefinitely by P'yŏngyang on March 19, 1978, on the score that the joint U.S.-ROK military exercises "strained North-South relations to an extreme extent," making the holding of meetings impossible.

While the precise reasons for the DPRK refusal to continue the South-North dialogue could be subjected to varying interpretations, there could be no doubt as to where the initiative in closing off discussion had lain. Moreover, P'yŏngyang's stated reasons were clearly specious. If the anti-communist laws, the enactment of the Yushin Constitution, the detention of certain anti-communist liberals, and joint U.S.-ROK military exercises made discussions impossible, how did the DPRK come to enter into discussions with the Pak government in the first place? Prior to 1971, Kim Il-sŏng and other DPRK spokesmen had repeatedly claimed that the Pak government was a "fascist regime," totally repressive and controlling its people through sheer force. On more than one occasion, North Korean leaders had insisted that they would negotiate with anyone *except* Pak —inviting an overthrow of the ROK President. Then abruptly the DPRK position changed.

Up to 1979, the official North Korean posture appeared to revert to one close to that of the pre-1971 period. It is highly instructive to read closely Kim Il-sŏng's major speech entitled "Let us Step Up Socialist Construction Under the Banner of the Chuch'e Idea," delivered on the 30th anniversary of the founding of the DPRK, September 9, 1978 (FBIS, 1978). One significant section of the speech had as its sub-head, "Let Us Smash the 'Two Koreas' Plot and Peacefully Reunify the Country." Kim commenced by denouncing "the American imperialists" for having made the "two Koreas" policy the basis of their strategy toward Korea, and in language typical of his speech, asserted, "Under the aegis of the American imperialists and Japanese reactionaries, the South Korean puppet clique overtly made the plot of national partition their policy and, raving about 'simultaneous UN membership' and 'cross recognition,' are making frantic efforts to create 'two Koreas'."

We must smash this plot, Kim continued, via the united strength of the entire Korean people, and after seeking to distinguish the Korean problem from the German problem (Germany was party to a war of aggression and a defeated nation), he remarked, "if Korea remains divided, this will be a constant menace to peace in Asia and the rest of the world."

After these somewhat threatening words, Kim reiterated his long-standing statement that reunification should be solved in a peaceful way, and insisted that the DPRK was keeping the door open for dialogue at all times—for conversations with the United States, and with the South Korean authorities and political parties, too. (Here, he carefully separated the two entities.) He then proceeded to outline what appeared to be his conditions for a resumption of the dialogue. He began by asserting that both parties should proceed "from the right position," not using discussions "as a means for rigging up 'two Koreas'." In other words, the dialogue should commence from premises acceptable to the DPRK. Brushing aside Pak's proposal for South-North economic cooperation, Kim asserted that "if the South Korean authorities sincerely want a dialogue and collaboration with us, they should change their policy of national division for a reunification policy and their anti-communist policy for a policy of alliance with communism (FBIS, 1978)."

Reunification must be based upon "great national unity," Kim stated, and among other things, this required both sides to refrain from imposing their ideas—communist or capitalist—upon the other, but putting forward a common idea—the national idea—and on this basis, achieving unity. The parties of the North should be allowed to operate in the South, and the parties of the South could operate in the North, with each side "fully opening its society to the other" and realizing a many-sided collaboration in political, economic, cultural, and military fields.

Having set forth this wholly impractical scheme, Kim launched into a vitriolic denunciation of the ROK which indicated his real expectations with respect to "great unity." South Korea, he asserted, has at present "the most despotic and infamous fascist rule unprecedented in history." After continuing in this vein for several sentences, the key line was inserted: "Unless the South Korean society is democratized, its people cannot free themselves from their present situation where they can enjoy no rights and, moreover, national union cannot be achieved nor can the way to peaceful reunification be found."[11]

And how was this "democratization" to take place? First, the Yushin Constitution should be abolished, all anti-communist laws annulled, together with the national security law and "other fascist laws." After demanding that full political freedom be restored, Kim continued, "The Revolutionary Party for Reunification and other clandestine political parties should be legalized, and Korean organizations and patriotic persons struggling abroad for the democratization of South Korean society and the independent, peaceful reunification of the country should be permitted to return to South Korea as they wish and engage in free political activities (FBIS, 1978)."

Calling upon the South Koreans to form a united front against "the fascist forces of dictatorship," and the United States to discontinue "its colonial rule in South Korea," withdrawing all military forces, Kim then remarked:

If the United States truly wants peace and Korea's peaceful reunification, it should naturally contact the government of the DPRK to seek for a way to solve the Korean question peacefully. We have already made a proposal for negotiations with the United States and are making efforts to this end. The question is, whether the United States sincerely wants to conduct negotiations with us or not, and, in case it wants to, whether it means to negotiate for a single Korea or for 'two Koreas.' If it abandons its wrong stand to divide our country into 'two Koreas' and assumes the right attitude to bring about Korean reunification, we will start talks with it at any time and settle all necessary problems. Then the United States will be able to withdraw its hands from the Korean question without impairing its own honor, and this will accord with the interests of both our people and the people of the United States.

A few paragraphs later, moreover, the fierce Kim re-appeared:

In pursuance of their invariable wild designs to bring the world under their domination, the American imperialists are stepping up war preparations while fooling peoples of the world by putting up the specious sign of 'peace'. They continue with armament expansion under the sign of restrictions on nuclear weapons and go on with military intervention under the sign of 'easing tensions'. As their economic crisis deepens and their position gets more strained, the imperialists intensify their maneuvers for aggression and war (FBIS, 1978).

In this speech from which we have quoted extensively, and many others of a similar nature, there was little to warrant optimism about the future of South-North relations. The DPRK line was essentially that until the Pak government had carried out a series of "reforms" as directed by Kim *or* that government had been overthrown by a united front of "democratic people," dialogue was futile. And surely hypocrisy reached a new level when Kim blandly asserted, "To guarantee the freedom of activity for political parties and public organizations is the most elementary requirement of democracy. In the northern half of the republic, different political parties and public organizations are now operating freely, enjoying legal rights (FBIS, 1978)." Apart from the sheer audacity of such a statement, it reveals how difficult political cooperation between communist and non-communist Korea would be at this stage.

A new turn in South-North relations began on January 19, 1979, when Pak proposed that talks on peace and reunification between the two Koreas be resumed "at any time, any place and any level, without any preconditions." In June 1978, when Pak had proposed private-level economic discussions between South and North, the DPRK had immediately rejected the idea, but this time, Kim Il-sŏng caused an affirmative response to be issued in the name of the Central Committee of the Democratic Front for the Reunification of the Fatherland.

In that response, the DFRF put forth four provisions: a re-affirmation by both sides of the principles contained in the joint declaration of July 1972 on February 1; the immediate cessation of "calumnies and slanders" against each other, officially or in private; an end of all hostile military actions as of March 1, and the cessation of weapon shipments from outside the peninsula, arms reinforcement, military operations, and the construction of military positions in frontline areas; finally, a conference in either P'yŏngyang or Seoul on September 1 that would include representatives of all political parties and public organizations in the North and South—including the president of the Democratic-Republican Party (Pak Chŏng-hi).

On the surface, this appeared to be a promising development. In reality, it was a step forward only when measured against the nearly 6 years of non-communication that had preceded it; it was actually a step backward from the 1972-1973 negotiations and dialogue. To understand this fact, one must be familiar with the history of the Democratic Front for the Reunification (Unification) of the Fatherland, and the final proposal in the DFRF response to Pak's offer (Scalapino and Lee, 1972: 388-390ff). That organization was actually founded on June 25, 1949, with some 700 delegates meeting in P'yŏngyang purporting to represent 71 "patriotic parties and social organizations" from both North and South Korea. Its central purposes were "achieving the restoration of national territory, completing Korean unification and independence by forcing the withdrawal of American forces and the destruction of Syngman Rhee's puppet government." One of the participants has asserted that the organization from the beginning was totally dominated by the key leaders of the Workers' Party, with Kim Il-sŏng and other prominent communists of the period heading the leadership. The first declarations of the DFRF, incidentally, were to assert among other things, that acceptance of the USSR proposal of 1948 for the withdrawal of all foreign forces would have made it possible for the Korean people to have resolved their internal problems without external involvement; that the government of the Democratic People's Republic of Korea, having been duly constituted and elected, received the support of the great majority of the Korean people; and that the American imperialists and reactionary Korean elements had established a puppet government in the south, consisting of Korean reactionaries and national traitors, to pursue the policy of dividing Korea (Scalapino and Lee, 1972:389, note 16).

The proposal of unification via a conference of all political parties and public organizations, North and South, has an even longer history. Its foundations may be said to have been laid at the meeting of U.S., Soviet, and allied foreign ministers in Moscow in December 1945. The Moscow Agreement provided for a 5 year joint trusteeship over Korea, with the establishment of a provisional Korean government via the participation of democratic political parties and organizations. All Korean parties violently rejected the Moscow Agreement, even the communists, until they were forced into line. But in addition, U.S. and USSR representatives to the Joint American-Soviet Commission on Korea could never agree upon a definition of "democratic parties and organizations," and for good reasons. Colonel General T. F. Shtykov, head of the Soviet delegation to the Joint American-Soviet Commission repeatedly argued in the spring of 1946 that in North Korea, a wide range of "democratic parties and organizations" now existed, whereas in the South, oppression of such groups proceeded under American-Rhee aegis (Scalapino and Lee, 1972:366). Indeed, a number of parties and front organizations had been created in the North, each of them under the control of the communists.

From this point on, the communists never ceased to forward the concept of unification via a union of all existing "democratic" parties and organizations. The American-Russian Joint Commission adjourned in May 1946, having never gotten beyond a fierce debate over this problem.

Following the Korean War, the DPRK leadership carried on with precisely the same theme. At the Geneva Conference of

1954, for example, Nam Il, DPRK foreign minister, called for an All-Korea Commission, composed of an equal number of North and South Koreans, representative of all political parties and social organizations, to determine the conditions leading to unification, meanwhile promoting economic and cultural exchange between the North and South.

The communist strategy has thus been consistent and from their standpoint, eminently sensible: preserve complete control of politics in the North via the Korean Workers' Party, but at the same time, maintain the fiction of political pluralism and united front operations, using the Democratic Front for the Reunification of the Fatherland for these purposes; then, insist upon full representation of all political factions in the South, knowing that the genuine political pluralism within the ROK can be exploited. Thus, even if the southern population is twice that of the north, and the communist movement there is practically non-existent, it may be possible to forward southern disunity and build a communist movement, taking advantage of the ROK political system.

Against this background, the events of early 1979 become more understandable. It is quite possible that neither the South nor the North expected much to come from the reopened discussions, and that both were responding to a variety of international pressures and opportunities. In any case, when delegates from North and South met at Panmunjom on February 18, the former came as members of the Democratic Front for the Reunification of the Fatherland, the latter as members of the previously established South-North Coordinating Committee. And while initial agreement was reached upon reopening the telephone hot line, on the crucial issue there has been no agreement to date.

The North Koreans have insisted that the SNCC be replaced by a southern counterpart of the DFRF, looking toward a bigger gathering to be called an "All-Korea Conference," composed of representatives of all parties and organizations, North and South, which shall determine the future structure of a reunified Korea. They currently assert that they will talk only with "representatives from all walks of life." (Does this sound familiar?) The South Koreans have insisted that negotiations can only be conducted successfully by "responsible authorities," that is to say, individuals who acquire their position on a body like the SNCC through official appointment of their respective governments. They accuse the North of abandoning the joint agreement of 1972.

As of the early summer of 1979, renewed negotiations had broken upon this rock. After five meetings, the North sent no representatives to a sixth session called by the South in late March. Meanwhile, disagreement also extended to the question of participation as a unified North-South team in the international ping-pong tournament held in P'yŏngyang. In the end, the North refused to issue visas to South Korean players when Seoul rejected the Northern proposal. The hot line is once again dead, although both sides seek to communicate with each other via various means. Recently, the DFRF sent several hundred letters to prominent South Koreans, including leaders of political, religious, and social organizations, outlining their proposals and soliciting support.

At the same time, the Voice of the Revolutionary Party for Reunification continues its attacks upon Pak, the ROK government, and the United States. A typical example is contained in a broadcast of May 13, 1979:

> With no sophistry can the U.S. imperialists justify the nation-selling acts of the Pak Chŏng-hi ring and the permanent stationing of U.S. troops in South Korea (FBIS, 1979a).

The official communist press in North Korea is currently no less harsh. In a *Nodong Sinmum* article of May 16, a commentator wrote:

> As all facts show, South Korea today is under a harsh fascist rule unprecedented in history. The South Korean authorities have established the fascist yushin system and (are) ruthlessly trampling the basic rights of the masses of people through numerous fascist evil laws including the Anticommunist Law, the National Security Law,

the State of Emergency and the Emergency measures. They have reduced the livelihood of the people to a state of the greatest misery and are suppressing the patriotic people and democratic figures who demand democracy and reunification of the fatherland (FBIS, 1979b).

A compromise may ultimately be worked out enabling the negotiations to resume, but the prospects for significant agreement on the range of issues confronting the two governments are not bright.

Against this background, for the United States to engage in an official dialogue with the DPRK without the presence of the ROK would be highly irresponsible. Had it been undertaken earlier, as some writers urged, it would almost certainly have stiffened the DPRK resistance to any form of bilateral discussions with the South, and stiffened communist terms for any future settlement as well. Kim would rightly have seen it as a major victory for his stone-walling tactics.

These factors remain valid. U.S. bilateral negotiations with the DPRK at this point would not only produce a virtual rupture in U.S.-ROK relations, raising to new heights questions about our credibility and even our basic morality, but they would also create a profound sense of insecurity throughout Asia. Quite properly, therefore, the Carter administration has repeatedly made it clear that it will enter into no negotiations with the DPRK without the approval or participation of the ROK.

In conjunction with President Carter's visit to Korea, June 30-July 1, 1979, he and President Pak jointly proposed a three-way meeting among the senior officials of the United States, South Korea and North Korea aimed at "reducing the threat of war" and "ultimately promoting the reunification of Korea." P'yŏngyang rejected the proposal, and while some observers remain optimistic that the North will ultimately reconsider, the past record is not encouraging. Up to date, Kim Il-sŏng has seemed determined to resist anything approaching realism with respect to the Korea issue, demanding some form of rapid unification under a formula not only promising the communists full political and military equality with the South, but also guaranteeing to them the type of rights in the South that they could not conceivably permit in the North unless they were prepared to abandon the communist system, Kim's rhetoric notwithstanding. This road leads nowhere.

One need not search far to discover why Kim is so concerned about what he calls "the two Koreas plot." Increasingly, a variety of countries have had to recognize that two Koreas exist, that peaceful reunification is not feasible in the near term at least, and that a reduction of tension demands a recognition of both governments as *de facto* states. At the end of 1978, South Korea maintained diplomatic relations with a total of 105 countries while North Korea had such ties with 93 nations, indicating clearly that a number of states recognized both. Since even the Soviet Union and certain East European states have appeared to be moving in this direction in the recent past, Kim is deeply worried, seeing the policies of the DPRK far less firmly supported than previously. To this aspect of the situation, we shall return shortly.

The position of the ROK and Pak Chŏng-hi on the question of South-North relations and general foreign policy is also a matter of deep concern to Kim, and legitimately so, since on this front, South Korea is both realistic and enlightened. While calling repeatedly for a resumption of South-North discussions, the ROK government has also proposed such interim measures as a non-aggression pact between the two governments and a consultative body for the promotion of South-North economic cooperation.[12] Beyond this, on June 23, 1973, Pak announced that he would accept DPRK participation in international organizations with the ROK, including joint admission into the United Nations, and that the Republic of Korea was willing to recognize all nations on the basis of the principles of reciprocity and equality, thereby opening the door to relations with communist states. Subsequently, the ROK government made it clear that it would not object to American and Japanese recognition of the DPRK, if the DPRK would agree to recognition by the USSR and the PRC of the ROK.

None of the steps, were they to materialize, would foreclose the possibility of the eventual reunification of Korea. On the contrary, they would enable patient, step-by-step developments through persistent negotiations in the atmosphere of greatly reduced tension. They represent the only possible route to peaceful reunification and they should have the strongest support of the United States.

Nevertheless, as has been indicated, there are no signs at present that North Korea is prepared to accept this approach. For some time, the tactics of the DPRK have been oriented in a different direction, namely, that of seeking to drive the United States and Japan away from the ROK. At more or less the same time as Kim Il-sŏng was withdrawing his representatives from various South-North discussions, he and his spokesmen were seeking an opening to the United States—the mutual pledge rejecting external interference in Korean affairs notwithstanding. The first overture came in the spring of 1974 when the DPRK Supreme People's Assembly urged that direct peace talks between Americans and North Koreans take place. Almost certainly, this was a reaction to the earlier willingness of the United States to engage in peace negotiations with North Vietnam over the protests of the South Vietnamese. Could this be a more promising route from P'yŏngyang's standpoint than the South-North dialogue?

Despite the absence of any indication that the United States was interested in bilateral negotiations, these overtures continued, and on the eve of Carter's advent to the presidency, they were accelerated, no doubt with the hope that a new president—one known to have reservations about past U.S.-ROK relations—might be amenable. Thus, a personal letter from Kim Il-sŏng to President-elect Carter dated December 20, 1976, was delivered by Prime Minister Bhutto stating that the DPRK was ready to negotiate a peace agreement with the United States, and that as negotiations progressed, "some other countries concerned" might be able to take part—a scarcely comforting sop to the South Korean government. The use of Pakistan as intermediary was a striking reflection of the China model, and may have come as a suggestion from Beijing.

This initiative was quickly followed up by Kim. In January 1977, he told a Japanese Dietman that he had opened the door so that a dialogue with the United States could commence. Later that month, Minister of Defense O Chin-u carried a personal letter from Kim to Bhutto thanking him for his assistance, and indicating that the DPRK intended to push forward with its efforts to negotiate with the United States. The following month, Ho Tam, DPRK Foreign Minister in a letter to Secretary of State Vance, urged bilateral talks, and in June, once again, Kim Il-sŏng in an interview with a *Le Monde* editor, asserted that discussions with Washington could commence if the United States withdrew its troops and began a review of its relations with South and North Korea. Carter was also invited to visit P'yŏngyang.

The United States' position regarding negotiations with North Korea remained consistent throughout this period. Spokesmen asserted that talks with North Korea could commence at any time but that South Korea must be a party to such discussions. The Ho Tam letter remained unanswered. However, unofficial contacts were no longer formally discouraged. On March 8, 1977, restrictions on travel by Americans to North Korea were lifted, and in the spring of 1979, the U.S. government, indicating that sports were a private matter, interposed no objections to American ping-pong players participating in the international tournament held in P'yŏngyang, accompanied by some U.S. journalists. Yet the current impasse remains between Kim's insistence upon bilateral discussions excluding the ROK, and the United States' position that any discussions to which it is a party must be at least trilateral in nature.

On this issue, the United States must not retreat. To undertake bilateral negotiations with P'yŏngyang under any conditions would have a devastating effect upon U.S.-ROK relations. Whether intended or not, it would be a clear signal of abrogating a solemn pledge, and it would be interpreted by the overwhelming majority of Koreans of whatever political allegiance as a betrayal. It would also be evidence to each of the major powers within the area of a continued confusion and irresolution on the part of the United States. Thus, it would abet instability—the type produced by increased North Korean intransigence, and by pressure upon Japan to move quickly—and prematurely—toward a "two Koreas" position, and by fortifying the current Chinese position in support of the DPRK.

There is no need to prohibit private cultural contacts between Americans and North Koreans, but everyone concerned should be fully aware of the DPRK objective in such events, namely, the establishment of unofficial ties with the U.S. as a step toward full diplomatic recognition. Via this means, it hopes to mount pressure upon U.S. policymakers and the American community at large, especially the intellectuals and journalists, to shift U.S. policy on Korea. Indeed, DPRK policy in the immediate future will concentrate on cultivating and exploiting all types of unofficial North Korean-American ties. Thus, in any schedule of cultural contacts, care should be taken to insist upon some balance—including the participation of individuals other than those merely representative of the left. Until the foreign policies of the DPRK are explicitly changed in the direction of peaceful coexistence, moreover, U.S.-DPRK trade and economic intercourse should not be sanctioned. Any unilateral concessions to P'yŏngyang can only deter the cause of peace and stability on the Korean peninsula.

VIII. KOREA AND THE MAJOR POWERS

I s there any possibility in the meantime that the major powers concerned about Korea other than the United States will indicate approval or sympathy with a realistic, peaceful solution—one accepting the current status-quo while encouraging the reopening of a South-North dialogue?

The relations between the Republic of Korea and Japan combine intimacy and acrimony, vital interests, and yet suspicions born out of centuries of intermittent hostility. Few peoples of Asia have been bound more closely together by culture, economics, and politics than the Koreans and Japanese. Modern Korean nationalism, however, quite naturally chose Japan as its primary target, given the period of Japanese dominance and colonialism imposed upon Korea, extending over nearly half a century. On both sides, racial prejudices exist along with Korean memories, or images of mistreatment. On the other hand, the Japanese impact on modern Korea has been extensive and continuous—in education, legal institutions, and above all, in recent times, in the economic sphere.

At present, Japan is the most important investor and trading partner with the Republic of Korea, a record built almost entirely since 1965 when diplomatic relations between the two countries were reestablished. As indicated earlier, nearly 60 percent of all foreign investment in South Korea comes from Japan. Indeed, Japanese influence in this respect has long been a political issue within Korea; and in 1978, two-way trade between ROK and Japan reached nearly $8.6 billion, over 22 percent more than the $7 billion U.S.-ROK trade. Yet in contrast to the $1 billion surplus provided to South Korea by the latter trade, the South Koreans had a $3.3 billion deficit in their trade with Japan during 1978. The persistent trade deficit with Japan in recent years, as in the case of the United States, has been a matter of growing concern to Korean leaders, and the subject of continuous negotiations. Moreover, the Korean complaints are similar to those voiced by American entrepreneurs: Japanese markets are most difficult to penetrate because of Japanese trade policies, distribution methods, and industrial structure.

There have been other sources of tension. A territorial dispute has existed over a few rocky atolls in the Sea of Japan. More important, substantial differences over fishing rights have erupted from time to time, including one relating to Korean fishing in the waters off Hokkaido which riled relations in 1978 and 1979. Since World War II, moreover, some 600,000 Koreans have remained in Japan, most of them residing in the great Osaka and Tokyo metropolitan complexes, and often close to the bottom of the economic ladder. Naturally, this population has served as targets for DPRK and ROK recruitment efforts. In these drives, the North took an early lead. With substantial resources and a strong organization, the DPRK made the General Federation of Korean Residents in Japan *(Choch'ongyŏn)* a 200,000 member auxiliary. In addition, P'yŏngyang provided the funds for a "university" in Tokyo transmitting its political themes along with some basic education.

The General Federation has not only served as a propaganda outlet for the DPRK in Japan and elsewhere; it has also provided the means for the transmission of agents to South Korea. The man who killed President Pak's wife in an attempt to assassinate Pak, for example, had come to Seoul from Japan, and was affiliated with Choch'ongyŏn. Naturally, the ROK government has resented Japanese tolerance of the General Federation's activities, and for a time after the assassination effort, relations between Seoul and Tokyo were very strained.

However, the ROK government has not been inactive in Japan. Using its organization, *Mindan*, South Korea has sought to make inroads into the General Federation, partly by inviting members of that body to visit ancestral tombs and relations in the South, thereby conducting via Japan the "humanitarian program" that has not yet been approved via South-North negotiations. Moreover, the kidnapping of Kim Tae-jung in Tokyo was a Korean CIA operation, with political repercussions that reverberated through the Japanese Diet for years. For Japan, the intrusion of Korean politics onto its soil has been a recurrent source of trouble, sometimes with international implications.

On balance, the Japanese government has consistently tilted toward South rather than North Korea, for political and security as well as economic reasons. Periodically, however, high ranking Japanese officials have made statements alarming or irritating to the ROK government. Foreign Minister Kimura's statement a few years ago protesting joint U.S.-ROK military exercises produced a strong protest from Seoul, as did the more recent remarks of Foreign Minister Sunoda suggesting that the security of the ROK was not of great significance to Japan—remarks later "interpreted" to mean that the security problem on the Korean peninsula had declined.

The South Korean government is aware of the fact that Japan's goal is a "two Korea" policy, and it does not object to such a policy over time, but it has recurrent suspicions that Japan may jump the gun, making premature and unilateral concessions to P'yŏngyang. Successive Japanese administrations have promised that they will not proffer diplomatic recognition to the DPRK until cross recognition is accepted by the PRC and USSR, but Seoul does not completely trust Tokyo on this matter. It is aware of the elements within the LDP, not to mention the leftist parties, anxious to move more rapidly toward legal recognition of North Korea. It knows that pressures in this regard might have been stronger has not Japan-DPRK economic relations declined against a record of extensive Japanese credit and unpaid North Korean obligations. There is some evidence now, however, that the P'yŏngyang government is in the process of straightening out its earlier economic mess, and is preparing to conduct another drive for stronger economic, political, and cultural ties with Japan. Thus, while the economic and political relations between the ROK and Japan are extensive, and include such institutions as joint ministerial conferences and interparliamentary meetings, a harmonious relationship can never be taken for granted, and Japanese policies toward the two Koreas may be subject to fluctuations.

It is imperative, therefore, that the United States and Japan work closely in consultation with each other on matters relating to Korea. There should be no further "shocks" from either side regarding Korean polices. Moreover, the policies of both nations should uphold the basic principles of cross-recognition of the two Koreas by the major states, admission of both to the UN and other international bodies, and peaceful coexistence on the Korean peninsula pending any agreement on peaceful unification.

Relations between the ROK and the USSR remain minimal, but with occasional hints of possible changes for the better. In major degree, this is a reflection of Moscow's problems with P'yŏngyang. Relations between the DPRK and the USSR have ranged from cool to hostile for many years, with a few interludes when the frost thawed slightly. The troubles started in the 1950s, focusing upon Moscow's efforts to intervene in the internal politics of North Korea in 1956, but probably relating to earlier pressures as well. Although there were several swings of the pendulum after that time, DPRK-USSR relations were never again based upon true cooperation and trust. After 1969, moreover, when Kim evidenced a persistent tilt toward Beijing, renewed deterioration of relations with Moscow unfolded.

Despite a welter of conflicting rumors, the evidence continues to suggest that P'yŏngyang's ties with Moscow are fragile, with no love lost on either side. Although Kim Il-sŏng did accept a Soviet decoration recently, one conferred upon him years ago, and has also met with a Soviet official—an action rare in recent times—he has not yet returned to Moscow, a trip oft-rumored about to take place, but not yet consummated. His last trips abroad in 1975 conspicuously included the PRC, Rumania, Yugoslavia, and Bulgaria, but not the USSR. Nor is there any evidence to suggest that the Soviet Union has been generous in economic aid. The DPRK continues to remain dependent upon the USSR for its more sophisticated military equipment, and for most industrial machinery, especially parts to keep earlier Soviet imports in operation. In addition, some plants may have been constructed with Russian assistance in recent years. On the other hand, past efforts to obtain major economic aid from the USSR do not appear to have been successful. More interesting is the fact that since 1978, at least, the PRC has furnished North Korea with more oil than has the Soviet Union.

During this same period, the USSR increasingly showed itself willing to permit South Koreans to enter the Soviet Union despite the vigorous protests of the DPRK. In August 1973, for example, 38 South Korean athletes were granted visas to attend the World Student Games, causing the North Koreans to refuse to come. Again, in September 1975, 16 South Koreans were admitted to participate in wrestling and weight-lifting competition. And in September 1978, the ROK Minister of Health and Social Affairs was permitted to attend an international health conference, with two South Korean journalists accompanying him. Most recently, in the spring of 1979, a formal overseas telephone line was opened between South Korea and the Soviet Union via the good offices of the British, followed by a similar line between the ROK and Bulgaria.

On the issues pertaining to reunification and North-South relations, the Soviet Union publicly continues to lend support to Kim Il-sŏng's position, but weakly. Soviet spokesmen call for the withdrawal of all U.S. forces from South Korea and to date they have contradicted none of Kim's proposals for reunification. Nonetheless, the Soviet delegation to the highly touted 30th Anniversary of the Founding of the DPRK was a remarkably low-level one, and the speech of its head, N.M. Matchanov, was extremely cautious and restrained.[13]

Further, in private conversations with American scholars and others, prominent Soviet citizens are critical of North Korea, especially the cult of exclusivism, combined with the official tilt toward China. They neither like nor trust Kim Il-sŏng.

From time to time, however, rumors emerge to the effect that North Korea and the Soviet Union are enroute to improving their relations, with specific illustrations sometimes cited. The most recent report of this type was to the effect that the Soviet Union had been permitted to use the port of Najin on the west coast of North Korea as a naval base, enabling additional Soviet assistance to Vietnam—Najin being a port never closed because of winter ice, unlike Vladivostok. This seemed dubious in view of the DPRK's support of Cambodia (Pol Pot) in the recent conflict, and in fact, the agreement related to the commercial use of the port. Both *Rodong Sinmun* and P'yŏngyang radio categorically denied that rights had been granted the USSR to use Najin or any other port as a naval base; this denial, moreover, was followed by a similar statement from Kim Il-sŏng himself in a conversation with UN Secretary-General Kurt Waldheim during the latter's visit to P'yongyang in the spring of 1979.

There is always the possibility that the Soviet Union will be tempted to shift its policies toward the DPRK as a result of the American-Chinese rapprochement, seeking to pursue its containment of the New New China in the north as well as in the south, and being prepared to pay more for this effort because of its concern over a possible PRC-U.S.-Japan united front against it. As yet, however, that has not occurred, and past reports that North Korea was maintaining a balance in its relations between the USSR and the PRC have been in-accurate. The tilt toward China, particularly since 1969, has been pronounced, and to Moscow, P'yŏngyang represents an ungrateful, even perverse ex-client state.

Does this augur well for ROK efforts to establish cultural, economic, and political ties with Eastern Europe and the Soviet Union? The answer is unclear at present, although recent trends have been generally conducive to that end. As has been noted, limited cultural contacts and communication facilities now exist. Some trade is also taking place between South Korea and Eastern Europe. Privately, many Soviet and Eastern European spokesmen indicate that in the long run, they expect and desire a German solution to apply on the Korean peninsula. In fact, they have no wish to see a change in the status-quo, and certainly not another conflict, given the likelihood that due to its cultural and geographic prox-imity, China will usually have paramount influence among foreign powers over North Korea.

Yet there are unquestionably limits to Soviet initiatives with respect to South Korea. To some extent, P'yŏngyang can play Beijing off against Moscow, and there is also the attitude of certain Eastern European countries to take into account. Moreover, the nature of future relations among the United States, China, and Japan—as we have noted—must be con-sidered. Any growth in Soviet-South Korean relations, there-fore, is likely to be subtle and incremental.

Before assessing the possibilities of U.S. policies in this connection, let us explore the policies and attitudes of the other major communist state toward the Korean issue. Are the relations between the People's Republic of China and the DPRK equally as complex as those between the USSR and the DPRK?[14] Possibly—but the preponderant weight of evidence suggests that for the past decade at least, Beijing and P'yŏng-yang have effected a much closer relation than has prevailed between Moscow and P'yŏngyang. Close ties with the Chinese were first forged during and after the Korean War although there were some rocky periods. In the early stages of the

Sino-Soviet cleavage, after some efforts to achieve a "neutral" status, Kim and his supporters moved into the ideological camp of Mao Zedong. During the height of the Cultural Revolution, Kim was attacked in Beijing posters, attacks later ascribed to leftists. There were also stories of border clashes over certain boundary issues.

One of Zhou Enlai's first major diplomatic offensives, however, after he regained control of foreign policy, was directed toward the North Koreans. His success is evidenced by the closeness of DPRK-PRC relations since that time, and the North Korean use of post-Cultural Revolution PRC foreign policy as a model in many respects. Like the Chinese, the North Koreans began to cultivate the Third World, turning outward; then they experimented—rather unfortunately, as it turned out—with an additional turning outward for industrial modernization, although this came earlier than the full-fledged PRC commitment; finally, they sought to cultivate the United States and Japan, albeit with different motives than those of the PRC in mind. Only in refusing to condemn publicly "hegemonism," and thereby risking the open repudiation of the USSR has the DPRK diverged from the PRC position in recent years.

It might thus be assumed that the PRC has had more leverage over the DPRK than has had the USSR in recent years. This, together with other factors, has led to an optimism in some American circles that the Chinese leaders would be of considerable assistance in helping to reduce tension and inducing peaceful coexistence on the Korean peninsula, a view that has been repeatedly communicated to South Korean leaders. To date, that judgment has proven to be overly optimistic, as in the case of so many other American assessments of the PRC and U.S.-PRC relations.

It is true that at an early point in American-Chinese discussions leading to detente, certain Chinese leaders appeared to indicate that the Korean problem was susceptible to resolution, and that they were prepared to lend assistance so that conflict might be avoided. Later, moreover, the Chinese were of some help in connection with the 1973 United Nations compromise on the Korean issue. One point is clear: like the Russians, the Chinese do not want war on the Korean peninsula at this time, recognizing how disastrous such a conflict would be for them as well as for all others.

Some Americans have argued that, privately, the PRC leaders want American military forces to remain in South Korea despite their public statements to the contrary. This may be true, but it has to be accepted on faith—in every private conversation of recent times, authoritative Chinese have championed American withdrawal, arguing that the issues can and should be handled by the Koreans alone.

It may be correct to assert that Kim Il-sŏng's recent acceptance of Pak's proposal for a renewed dialogue came in part because of Chinese suggestions, following Carter-Deng conversations on Korea in January 1979. But what are the Chinese analyses being presented to the North Koreans? Do they indicate the possibility of getting acceptance by the United States of the DFRF and of obtaining U.S. negotiations with the DPRK? Whatever the advice, little has been accomplished thus far in North-South negotiations except a sparring for propaganda advantage.

Meanwhile, the PRC has publicly given the DPRK staunch, seemingly unequivocal support in recent years. When Kim went to Beijing in April 1975, just after the collapse of the South Vietnamese government, he induced the Beijing government to recognize the DPRK in a joint communique as "the sole legal sovereign state of the Korean nation," and to couple its position on Korea with its position on Taiwan, a linkage which was to be repeated on many occasions subsequently.[15]

In contrast to Moscow, moreover, Beijing sent a very high level delegation to the 30th Anniversary celebration in P'yŏngyang in August 1968 headed by Deng Xiaoping. In a major address at the Hamhung city stadium, before a huge audience, Deng made the following remarks on reunification and the U.S. role in South Korea:

The reunification of Korea is the national aspiration of the Korean people in both the North and the South. No schemes to create 'two Koreas' in an attempt to perpetuate the division of Korea will ever succeed. The reunification of Korea will certainly become a reality. The Chinese people have always closely followed the just struggle of the Korean people to unify their fatherland, firmly support President Kim Il-sŏng's three principles and five-point program for the independent and peaceful reunification of Korea, firmly support the just position of the Korean people in demanding the disbandment of the 'UN command' and the complete withdrawal of the U.S. aggressor forces with their weapons and equipment from South Korea.[16]

Has U.S.-PRC "normalization" shifted Deng's views and those of other Chinese leaders? As indicated earlier, the Chinese may have suggested negotiations to the North Koreans. Insofar as public statements are concerned, however, there has been no retraction, or seeming modification of earlier positions as yet. In Japan, Deng publicly suggested that he saw no sign of military tension on the Korean peninsula, and is reported to have privately indicated that the time was not ripe for any changes in China's Korea policies. In private conversations of early 1979, Deng and others have stayed with their demand for American troop withdrawal and suggested that the U.S. must become a party to negotiations— presumably with the DPRK—but in a *triangular* context? Deng also indicated to Senator Jacob Javitz that he had a "Chinese solution" to the Korean problem, namely, a Korean Federation in which both sides retained economic and political autonomy. But this "Chinese solution" is remarkably like the first phase of Kim Il-sŏng's "solution," that of a "Koryo Confederation," Koryo being the ancient name for Korea.

In sum, the Chinese position remains essentially that of the DPRK on the crucial issues. The thesis of some American scholars that the PRC diverged from the DPRK on the issue of *peaceful* reunification and had applied pressure successfully in April 1975 to get Kim to accept this concept is ill-founded. The term "peaceful reunification" is one that has been used consistently by the North Koreans, including Kim, for a number of years. He did not have to be coerced into accepting it particularly since he has pursued a modified Vietnam formula in his plans for the "liberation" of South Korea for some time, and if he were to elect a more adventurous path, one can be certain that, as in the case of the Korean War of 1950, P'yŏngyang would allege that the initiative lay with Seoul. It is true that while in Beijing, Kim spoke in relatively belligerent terms about support for the South Korean people in their rebellion against the ROK government. On this point, however, there has been no retreat, nor any sign that the Chinese sought to turn Kim from a Vietnam strategy.

It may be correct, however, to assert that given its close ties with the DPRK, the PRC is in a position to play a greater role in working toward a resolution of the Korean problem than others, should it so choose. Yet, like Moscow, Beijing claims strict limits on its leverage with P'yŏngyang. The geographic position of the DPRK, fronting as it does on China's Manchurian industrial centers, makes it vital for the PRC to keep North Korea aligned. Recently, there have been rumors that the boundary issues between the PRC and DPRK earlier reported to have erupted in hostilities during the Cultural Revolution have reemerged, creating severe strains. However, Hua Guofeng in his conversation with Waldheim, strenuously denied that there were any differences between Beijing and P'yŏngyang. (There is no report that he made such a statement regarding relations with Moscow.) It should also be reiterated that the DPRK has officially thrown its backing to the Chinese-supported Pol Pot Cambodian government, flying in the face of strong Vietnamese and Soviet resentment. Further, it provided an additional home for Prince Sihanouk in 1979—a man rumored to be China's ace in the hole should the wheels of fortune, or more properly misfortune—make it possible for him to return to Cambodia.

Whatever the future may hold, moreover, the PRC government has made extremely limited overtures thus far in the direction of acknowledging the ROK. No cultural contacts have been permitted. Some indirect trade takes place via Hong Kong, and recently, the Chinese have signalled their interest in expanded trade—possibly the most encouraging development thus far. In the late spring of 1979, the PRC also indicated that certain Korean families living in Manchuria wishing to be repatriated to South Korea could depart if accepted, another slight crack in a door totally closed to that point.

Given these facts, certain and uncertain, what policies should the United States pursue with respect to the major Communist states on the Korea issue? First, it should be made clear that the Korean problem is regarded as one of great importance, not only to the Korean people but to the peace and security of the world. It should be made equally clear that, in the U.S. view, the current foreign policies of the DPRK are productive only of rising tension and the threat of conflict, while those of the ROK aim at peaceful coexistence and a realistic approach to the issue of reunification. It should also be stressed that policies toward the Korean peninsula cannot but be linked to the general climate of U.S. political-strategic relations with both China and Russia. In addition, the United States should stand ready to respond favorably to those actions of either party that forward the cause of Korean stability and peace.

It is certainly reasonable to continue to call for a multi-lateral major power discussion on the Korean problem while engaging in private, bilateral conversations with Beijing and Moscow, and encouraging the Japanese government to do likewise. The responsibilities of all nations historically involved in the Korean peninsula, as well as those falling upon the two Korean states, cannot be evaded. Each of the major states of the region plays a critical role in providing economic and military assistance to the two Koreas, and providing them also with political legitimacy and cultural outlets. The thesis that the issues pertaining to Korea can be resolved by Seoul and P'yŏngyang alone is fictional, although the responsibility of the primary actors remains paramount.

While reiterating the importance of all parties' responsibility and participation, U.S. continued willingness to participate in triangular discussions involving both the DPRK and the ROK should be indicated, providing there are no preconditions for such discussions. If triangular discussions do subsequently ensue, as some observers believe possible, the United States should engage in regular consultation with Japan, and above all, with the Republic of Korea. The recent establishment of bilateral U.S.-ROK meetings at the State Department-foreign office level is highly appropriate in this light. There must be no repetition of the disastrous Paris negotiations on Vietnam which resulted in private negotiations between Washington and Hanoi leading to the estrangement and ultimate destruction of South Vietnam. And no one should assume that those negotiations will not be recalled, especially by Koreans, even though the circumstances are very different.

In conclusion, two points are worthy of reemphasis. Today, the Republic of Korea is an important nation in its own right, and the United States should now recognize that fact, discarding completely the older notion of Korea as an adjunct to our Japan policy. It is also a nation possessing increasing pride and confidence, anxious to pursue its own path with emphasis on self-reliance. As in the case of Japan, its economic successes have provided the impetus for a new nationalism. This development is not without its paradoxes, for the older legacy of dependence upon the United States, particularly upon American military power, remains—and with justification, given Korea's precarious geopolitical position. A similar phenomena, indeed, exists in Japan. U.S. relations with Korea must take cognizance of *both* the new and the old forces shaping Korean attitudes and policies, recognizing this as a transitional period, likely to be lengthy.

Secondly, and on a broader scale, American strategy in Asia cannot afford to rely primarily upon communist nationalism, valuable though that property is for certain purposes. Relations with those nations with which Americans have the greatest commonality of interests—economic, political, and strategic—must be given a general priority; otherwise, the

United States will be uniquely vulnerable to unpredictable shifts in intracommunist relations as well as to tactical changes in communist relations with noncommunist states. It is indeed true that the world has become vastly more complex since the so-called "cold war" years—and few want to return to that era. Changes in former policies are both required and desirable. But priorities and emphases are at least as essential as in the past, and neither "neutralism" nor a pure "balance of power" strategy will suffice for the United States.

Nor can the United States afford to pursue in the future the type of unilateral concessions that have sometimes characterized its policies in the recent past. Unilateralism can only lead to disillusionment, and a breakdown of the negotiatory process that alone holds hope for peace in our time. This period demands continuous consultation with those nations aligned with the United States, coupled with firmness and patience in dealing with erstwhile adversaries, together with an insistence upon reciprocity and accountability. Relations with both South and North Korea will serve as a litmus-paper test as to whether Americans have learned these elemental, yet critical lessons.

NOTES

1. Korean apprehensions were further heightened when passages purporting to be from the top secret Presidential Review Memorandum 10 were leaked by U.S. columnists Rowland Evans and Robert Novak in September 1977. According to their account, this memorandum reported that once U.S. land forces were out of Korea, the United States would have transformed its presence in Asia from a land-based posture to an off-shore posture, thereby providing the United States with "flexibility to determine at the time whether it should or should not get involved in a local war." Continuing, PRM 10 allegedly said "the risk of automatic involvement is minimized." This is precisely what Koreans fear, and represents a reason for ground troop withdrawal quite contrary to those issued in public. For the presentation of the Evans-Novak story in Korea, see *The Korea Herald*, September 9, 1977.

Earlier, on June 14, 1977, the *Herald* had published a story written by Don Oberdorfer of the *Washington Post* to the effect that the Carter withdrawal decision had been swiftly translated into policy with the most limited official review.

For a congressional evaluation that is also critical in part, see the report issued by Senators Hubert Humphrey and John Glenn entitled "U.S. Troop Withdrawal From the Republic of Korea," January 9, 1978 (95th Congress, 2nd Session) U.S. Government Printing Office, Washington, 1978.

2. This author, Han Ki-shik, and Han Sungjoo carried out a survey of all Korean students and academicians in the United States in 1967 which bore out these facts in a striking manner. It was made available in mimeograph form under the title "The Political Attitudes of Korean Students and Academicians in the United States," Berkeley, 1967.

3. The elections of February 27, 1973 resulted in the election of 73 DRP and 52 NDP candidates, with a small splinter group from the NDP, the Democratic Unification Party winning two seats and independents receiving 19 seats. Seventy-three members were appointed by the president and approved by the National Council for Unification, and they formed a separate parliamentary group, the Yujŏnghoe (Political Association for Revitalization).

4. The political events of 1974-1976 within South Korea were exceedingly complex, testifying both to the continuing dynamism of the internal political scene and to sensitivities of all Korean parties to the importance of international, especially American opinion. Government policies during this period were characterized by successive moderating and hardening measures, with the basic effort to maintain stability without having to resort to massive repression. Thus, some of the emergency decrees were repealed in August 1974 and prominent dissidents were allowed officially to register an organization openly dedicated to "the restoration of democracy" in early 1975. Student demonstrations, moreover, took place regularly without being suppressed. As an "answer" to the dissidents, another referendum on the constitution was held in February 1975, with voter turnout recorded as 80 percent, and approval scored at 74 percent. The opposition, however, denied the validity of these results, and more militant confrontations ensued, with the government toughening its position by 1976.

As of mid-1979, the DRP had 83 seats of the 154 elected places, with the NDP holding 68, the remaining being independents. However, the 77 appointees of the 231 member assembly could also be counted in the government camp.

5. An excellent study of the Chang Myŏn period is that of Han Sungjoo, *The Failure of Democracy in South Korea*, University of California Press, Berkeley, Los Angeles, London, 1974.

6. For various recent hearings, see *Human Rights in South Korea: Implications for U.S. Policy*, May 20-December 20, 1974, Joint Hearings Before the Subcommittee on Asian and Pacific Affairs and the Subcommittee on International Organizations and Movements, Washington, D.C., 1975; *Human Rights in South Korea and the Philippines*, Hearings Before the Subcommittee on International Organizations, Washington, D.C., 1976; *Human Rights in North Korea*, September 9, 1976, Hearings Before the Subcommittee on International Organizations, Washington, D.C., 1976 and *Investigation of Korean-American Relations*, Hearings Before the Subcommittee on Asian and Pacific Affairs, Washington, D.C., 1977.

7. For a succinct discussion of the role of American economic assistance, see David C. Cole, "Foreign Assistance and Korean Development," in David C. Cole, Youngil Lim, and Paul W. Kuznets, *The Korean Economy—Issues of Development*, Korean Research Monograph, No. 1, Institute of East Asian Studies, University of California, Berkeley, 1979.

8. According to a research paper "Korea: The Economic Race Between the North and the South," p. 4, published by the U.S. Central Intelligence Agency, National Foreign Assessment Center, in January 1978, grain production in South Korea increased at an average annual rate of only 2.1 percent since 1965, slightly above the 2 percent growth of the population, but all of the growth occurred after 1973, at a pace of almost 7 percent per year. In addition, see also Robert A. Scalapino and Chong-Sik Lee, *Communism in Korea*, Vols. I and II, University of California Press, Berkeley, 1972; and Joseph Sang-hoon Chung, *The North Korean Economy—Structure and Development*, Hoover Institution Press, Stanford, 1974.

9. A comprehensive review of this work is contained in Raymond D. Gastil (editor and principal author) *Freedom in the World-Political Rights and Civil Liberties 1978*, G. K. Hall, Boston, 1978.

10. A detailed discussion of the background of South-North relations is presented in the author's essay entitled "The Two Koreas-Dialogue or Conflict?" in William J. Barnds (ed.), *The Two Koreas in East Asian Affairs*, New York University Press, New York, 1976, pp. 60-122.

11. The original as transcribed says "situation when they enjoy no right."

12. For the official statements and speeches of the ROK government and of Pak Chŏng-hi, see various issues of *South-North Dialogue in Korea*, published by the International Cultural Society of Korea, Seoul. For those of the DPRK government and of Kim Il-sŏng, see various issues of FBIS, *Asia and the Pacific—Daily Report*, and the Joint Publication Research Series, *Translations on North Korea*.

13. A P'yongyang report of Matchanov's speech broadcast domestically, is to be found in FBIS, *Asia and the Pacific*, 15 September 1978, D 13-14.

A Soviet report, which was even more laconic, was carried in a Korean language broadcast from Moscow, transcribed in FBIS, *Soviet Union*, 20 September, 1978, M 1-2. Matchanov was quoted as having said, "In the future, the Soviet people will support the struggle for independent and peaceful national reunification." (M 2)

14. I have earlier presented my views on this subject in the essay entitled "The Two Koreas—Dialogue or Conflict?" in William J. Barnds (ed.), *op. cit.*, pp. 60-122 (pp. 102-107).

15. The Joint Communique is presented in English in *Peking Review*, May 2, 1975, pp. 8-11.

16. For a P'yŏngyang transcription of portions of Deng's speech in English, see FBIS, *Asia and the Pacific*, 13 September 1978, D 3-4. Additions are carried in *Ibid.*, 14 September, 1978, D 1-3. For a somewhat more lengthy account, see FBIS, *People's Republic of China*, 12 September 1978, A 11-12. The quotation is from *Ibid.*, A 12.

88

REFERENCES

BROWN, H. (1978) Address to the Los Angeles World Affairs Council (February 20). Made available by Department of Defense, Office of Assistant Secretary of Defense, Public Affairs section, Washington, D.C.

COLE, D.C., et al. (1979) The Korean Economy—Issues of Development. Korean Research Monograph, No. 1. Berkeley: Institute of East Asian Studies, University of California.

Foreign Broadcast Information Service (1978) Asia and the Pacific section (September 12)

——— (1979a) May 15.

——— (1979b) May 16. "The South Korean authorities cannot conceal (their) fascist, splittist, nation-selling nature by any means."

HALLORAN, R. (1977) "Seoul reports show a wide U.S. campaign." New York Times (December 30).

HAN, Sungjoo (1979) "South Korea 1978: The growing security dilemma." Asian Survey (January).

KIM, Dae Jung (1979) "We seek democracy." Newsweek International (April 9).

KIM, Il-Sŏng (1979) "New year's message." in Kulloja No. 1 (January). Translated in Joint Publications Research Service 73144 (April 3).

Korea Herald (1978) September 13

Korea Newsreview (1978) "G.I. pullout harms America's own interest." (September 30).

LIM, Youngil (1979) "Korea's trade with Japan and the U.S.: Issues and implications," 31-49 in Cole et al. (see reference above)

Nodong Sinmun (1979) "The history of the revolutionary struggle of our people in the history of the great victory of the *Chuch'e* idea." Joint Publications Research Service 073196 (April 11).

SCALAPINO, R. and C. LEE (1972) Communism in Korea, Vol. 1. Berkeley: University of California Press.

U.S. Central Intelligence Agency, National Foreign Assessment Center (1978) Korea: The Economic Race Between the North and the South (January).